Gash Boat

H.M.S Coventry 1939 — 1942

Jack Dusty's Story

Frank Chadwick

Gash Boat

H.M.S Coventry 1939 — 1942

Jack Dusty's Story

ISBN 0 906437 16 4

Published by
Western Isles Publishing Company Ltd
Stornoway

Foreword

I suppose one could say that fate played a part in the publication of this book. I first stepped on Shetland soil on the 1st of April 1964. Apart from being April Fools Day, it was also the day when I first met Frank Chadwick.

Frank and his wife, Lilian, were to be my hosts, or should I say 'guardians', over the next two years in the Hayfield Hotel, Lerwick. These were probably two of my most formative years and I was fortunate to have them cast a paternal eye over my daily life's adventures. To me at that time Frank appeared an 'old sage', and offered many words of wisdom on life in general, and in particular on the romantic relationships I formed on the islands.

Like many others, I was entertained and fascinated by Frank's wartime stories and tales of the *Coventry*. I look back with nostalgia at the many pleasant weekend evenings I spent listening to Frank telling these tales. Better people than I tried to cajole him into putting these down on paper before they disappeared, but I resigned myself that this would probably never happen. At that time I had no connections with publishing anyway.

Thirty-five years have passed since that first meeting, but I am lucky to still count Frank amongst my friends. To my astonishment one evening in his home at Hillhead he announced that he had put these tales down on paper and was now seeking to have them published. Not wishing to sound too enthusiastic, I agreed to look at the manuscript — really wishing to bounce it off my business colleagues. The decision was unanimous. You simply picked up this book and read it to the end, irrespective of the time of day or whatever else was pressing. It simply had to go into print.

The stories are true, but written in a fickle light-hearted vein. The reader should be well warned that the humour from the 'lower deck' can be infectious. For me all those nights spent in the Hayfield Hotel came flooding back. The tales, I know, could go on and on, but we had to draw a line somewhere and get a book into print. I know you will enjoy this book from cover to cover.

From the same pen, there are threats of a book on the Hayfield Hotel, but I for one will agree to publish it on the grounds that I can censor it as well.

I wish your pen many further years of work, Frank.

David Stephen

Preface

This is not meant to be an historic account, autobiography or anything of that breed. It is just a few reminiscences of the three years from August 1939 when I served as a supply rating on an old light cruiser with some of the finest shipmates a man could ever wish to know. I had to depend on the recording capability of my then young brain cells to bring back to me the events of times long past, so if the story does seem to ramble on a wee bit, the facts are there or thereabout. Some things we never forget although everybody does not remember them in the same way.

I have tried to keep the writing light and easy but if the reader (thank you kindly) should think the narrative to be rather flippant — well, that is the way we were then. If we had taken life seriously all the time we should have gone round the twist — as quite a few poor fellows did, and their Lordships were not too well disposed towards ratings who became 'bomb-happy'.

Although I started scribbling notes some years ago, it came about only recently that I began to think it was time to start putting things together (as the office girl said to the president) and I am forever grateful for the voluntary help and encouragement I received from our good friends Maurice and Glynis Williamson. Maurice started it all by taking us on trips to remote parts of the Shetland Islands where I felt compelled to search the horizon and the troubled waters around St. Magnus Bay, Ronas Voe, Point of Fethaland and Colla Firth vividly recalling that nightmare voyage in the Autumn of 1939 to Sullom Voe where this adventure really began and very nearly came to a tragic end soon afterward.

Later on, when I had mustered as many of the facts and figures as I could bring to mind and jotted them down in something resembling literary conformity, Glynis used up such spare time as she had to transfer my not very legible manuscript to her magical word processor, patiently and cheerfully making repeated alterations and additions as the story slowly progressed. Who could ask for better neighbours? I am also grateful to her brother Geoff Leask who performed computer wizardry producing a prototype book to let me see what could be achieved. I doubt if all the skill of my two key-tapping fingers would ever have got the work done even with the lovely new typewriter which our good pal Ian Duncan contributed as his effort to spur me on.

Thanks also to cousin James Burnett and all the other good friends and relatives who during the last few years have urged and exhorted me to commit some of my wartime and other memories to print, probably hoping that the written version would be easier to endure than the oft repeated yarns of a boring old man.

Most of all I owe everything to my long suffering, dearly loved wife Lilian who put up with me and all the years of tears and tantrums of the would-be author while forever prompting and inspiring me to keep on writing

After all, it was the good old *Coventry* which brought us together in the first place so there is a lot for which I have to be thankful.

* * *

Some time ago I enjoyed the company of an elderly gentleman who had retired from the Royal Navy with the rank of Captain(S) and it came up in conversation that I had been a supply petty officer serving on *H.M.S. Coventry* during the first three years of the Second World War.

I was astonished when he said that those six old anti-aircraft cruisers were alluded to in Admiralty circles as 'The Suicide Squadron'.

It might have caused a wry smile or two on the lower deck if we had known about that doubtful honour in 1941 or the next year but I do not think we would have paid it much attention because by that time we were somewhat of the opinion that the Wizards of Whitehall were not fully aware of the difference in elevation and bearing between their 'A' bracket and their mid-forearm socket.

Nobody appeared to deem it necessary to tell us anything. We had the idea that every move we made must be kept top secret, except from the Germans and Italians and all their agents in Egypt.

It was our common task to carry out the unglamorous, non-propaganda-worthy duties and not to ask the why or wherefore. This prompted the old hands who had seen it all before to remind us that we were only 'gash boats' after all and it served us right — we should not have joined!

In these pages I have tried to tell, while I can still remember, something of the insignificant, but to me rather proud story of a 'Jack Dusty's' wartime experience on board one of the Gash Boats.

I tried not to look. It was too awful to believe. Perhaps it was only a bad dream. That was it. When I opened my eyes it would not be there. But this is not a romantic novel and nightmares cannot be sent away at the author's command. Perhaps the reader will understand my feelings as the story unfolds.

I was twenty years of age in the summer of 1939, starry-eyed and still fired with zeal and youthful enthusiasm after two years in the Royal Navy.

I was one of a large family. My father had been a farmer until he got on his horse in 1914 and went away with a famous Yeomanry regiment to fight the Great War ('the war to end wars'). Like so many, he came home in 1918 to a world which had little to offer an ex-serviceman except a lot of talk about a land fit for heroes to live in and other such platitudes which were nice things to say at the time. He worked hard to keep a roof over our heads in those days of mass unemployment and no such thing as 'Social Security' but we had to move home from county to county to wherever work was to be found.

He detested officialdom and tried to convince us that all politicians, councillors and civil servants were poverty stricken has-beens who were only there for what they could get out of it because they were no good at anything else. He warned us to have nothing to do with lawyers who would charge you a fortune if they only said good morning and they would probably be wrong about that. Mother was a true blue dyed-in-the-wool Conservative and we were all nurtured to the strains of 'Land of hope and glory' or, as the children sang, 'Land of soap and water'.

Although I had never been within ninety miles of the coast and did not know what the sea looked like, I had always wanted to be a sailor from the time I was a boy, especially after my brother Jack became a stoker in 1932 and went away to serve his first commission in the Mediterranean Fleet, based at Malta on board the great battleship *H.M.S. Queen Elizabeth*, coming home three years later with a tan and a tattoo and lots of tales to tell. He also brought home a canary in a cage.

As soon as I was old enough I took his advice and applied to enlist for a period of twelve years, that being the minimum sentence, as a writer or a supply rating — you had to give a second choice just like a mail-order catalogue.

I was sent all sorts of encouraging literature by recruiting officers who probably went to the same training school as estate agents; they certainly knew how to spice things up. They did not tell me much about the actual job but gave details of officers' salaries up to the rank of Paymaster Commander, neglecting to mention that I would have about as much chance of becoming a member of the wardroom as of the Luton Girls Choir. I was a baritone, anyway.

When I went for my physical examination they gave me a very severe going over after learning that I had survived rheumatic fever at the age of eleven, a broken knee at sixteen and all sorts of ailments which young folks had to live with in the nineteen-twenties. In fact, the tests which I endured would have finished me off there and then if I **had** been suffering from any of the cardiac impairments the Doctor suspected. It did not leave me with much dignity either, especially when he appeared to be examining my back teeth from a more distant orifice. Perhaps they were looking for the lost chord!

With so many young men wishing to join, the Royal Navy could afford to be choosy. A few years later, they would have taken you if you were warm.

Not long after that ordeal I had to rise in the middle of the night and cycle ten miles followed by a long train journey — at my own expense — in order to take the educational test and personal interview. I seem to have put up a heck of a performance to get into this man's navy! 'Served me right', I was told.

Three months later I was advised that I had been accepted as a supply rating and very soon I was on my way to Portsmouth where I saw the sea for the first time in my life, after surviving a hazardous voyage through the dreaded London underground railway where I kept getting off at the same station I had just left. You could die of starvation down there!

It was the twenty-first of September nineteen thirty-seven. My education was about to begin.

At Portsmouth railway station a group of bewildered, gormless looking new entries were gathered together and marched to the old Portsmouth naval barracks with the official name of *H.M.S. Victory* where we were hounded into a large office and were ordered to complete all sorts of forms and documents which were quickly forgotten, if indeed they penetrated our intelligence at all. Then we were given a service number which we had to remember. I was made to shout out those details so many times during the next twelve years that I am sure I shall never forget them.

Our first meal was a fried herring which the petty officer ordered us to eat with our fingers using newspaper as a plate so as not to leave a fishy smell on the mess utensils. Somebody said, 'Food for thought'.

We had a fairly easy week of settling in, getting kitted up (from then on we would have to buy our own kit) learning how to splice, point and graft and assemble our own hammocks, and then learning what it was all about. We had more medical examinations, presumably to see if we had deteriorated since the last time, and dental treatment where I was painfully relieved of two good teeth which required only a bit of repair. The young dentists had to practise on somebody.

We were separated into classes — all supply ratings together — and given our proper mess billet which, to apply our kindest description, was a bit on the rough side. Ah well — for the next few months it was to be our home, be it ever so humble.

When the training officers were satisfied that we were now near enough sub-human we were put through two months of square-bashing under strict discipline with rifle shooting and bayonet drill trying to teach us how to be good soldiers or something. Needless to say, I never had cause to handle a rifle again nor was I included in any ceremonial parades.

The square-bashing was not too bad while it lasted and we were blessed with a decent, humorous petty officer of Scottish birth as a drill instructor. In the navy we were spared the degradation so beloved by the other services where the drill sergeant always appeared to be a sadistic moron whose duty it was to belittle and browbeat young trainees with the object of making them wish they had never enlisted. That sort of bully would not have lasted long at sea!

After the rifle drill came two months of crammed study in accountancy where I was taught to push a pen with great dexterity and to learn all manner of official gobbledygook which I never did manage to interpret. When I went to my first actual job the old supply chief petty officer said, 'Right, now you can forget all that stuff they told you at the school and learn to do it the right way and never let me catch you using a ready-reckoner — that's what you were given brains for'. Of course that was before the day of the pocket calculator. I wonder what he would have made of them!

I have often had good reason to remember that sound advice. I came to learn that the Royal Navy's method of accounting for stores and provisions was probably the most accurate example of double entry book-keeping you could use — provided you employ low paid, hard working, unprotesting pen-pushers, each one doing at least the work of two and not daring to stray from the book of rules. And, of course, you must not have any ideas about that horrible stuff called 'profit'.

Every item of stock from a tap washer to a tin of beans could be traced from the ship back to the dockyard store from where it came. All accounts were recorded in quantity and value. They must be accurately balanced and agree with the stock records every three months or else those order-worshipping pencil boatswains would want to know the reason why. Every Sunday the supply chief petty officer had to produce a document telling the Captain exactly what it had cost to run each department of the ship for the past week as well as the amount of stocks on hand which were supposed to be kept at a level of three months' requirements.

It drove many a chief to the rum bottle, but it worked. At least it satisfied our Lords and Masters the civil servants. May they be encouraged to go and multiply themselves!

The recruiting literature had portrayed the duties of a supply rating as distributing and accounting for all the ship's stores and catering. It did not tell me that I should also be expected to hump crates of tinned food or large barrels of rum or lime-juice or two-hundredweight size bags of flour or sticky demerara sugar, as well as keeping the offices and stores tidy and clean. Nor was I told I would be acting as lamp trimmer, which meant looking after all the oil burning emergency lighting throughout the ship including navigation and fighting lights. It said nothing about action stations when I should probably have to work in one of the magazines handling cordite and shell or that I might be called upon to perform all manner of duties for which I had received no training at all.

Supply ratings were part of the Accountant Division along with writers, cooks, officers' cooks and officers' stewards and our boss was the Paymaster Commander. Unlike the executive officers, paymasters did not talk down to their ratings but rather treated us as intelligent beings.

Ours was probably the most unglamorous branch of the Royal Navy. Instead of the 'square rig' worn by the sailors with bell-bottoms and dickies and things we had to be content with 'fore-and-aft' uniform with the peaked cap — generally referred to as the 'cardboard forecastle' with its insignificant red cap badge.

We rejoiced under two nicknames. If you worked in the central stores (nuts and bolts etc) you were called a 'deep sea ironmonger' while if you looked after victualling, catering and clothing you were a 'Jack Dusty'. I rather liked that name.

Despite my lowly position I remained full of the old 'Grenville, Hawkins, Raleigh and Drake' business and the gospel according to Saint Nelson.

My first seagoing draft came early in 1938 when I was sent to join the new submarine depot ship *H.M.S. Maidstone* fitting out at John Brown's yard in Clydebank and that was where my new life really began. A few months previously I had never been far from home and here was I away north and over the border in the land I had learned about only through song and story.

I was with the advance party sent there to record and store all the ironmongery coming into the ship several weeks before the remainder of the ship's company came aboard. 'Old Stripey', who was a leading supply assistant, was so called because he had been in the Royal Navy for long enough to earn three good conduct badges worn on the arm like sergeant's stripes and was therefore at least thirty years old. He and I found lodgings in Clydebank with a lovely family and soon got to know quite a few people

— friendly, hard working down to earth Scots. Alas, most of them were killed a few years later during the terrible blitz.

John Brown's yard — what a history that conjures up — was very busy at that time with a variety of ships under construction, including four small destroyers for the Argentine navy as well as the Cunard liner *R.M.S. Queen Elizabeth*, then the biggest ship in the world and what a credit to her creators.

The mighty *Queen Elizabeth* was on the stocks near to *H.M.S. Maidstone* and I watched her grow every day as I walked by. I still think there was never anybody who could build them like the Clydesiders.

It was all very heady stuff for a young country lad from the middle of England who had to join the navy to see the sea.

We left the Clyde in a gale and steamed down through the Irish Sea, around Land's End and on to Portsmouth — not the easiest of trips for a green young sprog especially as my first day at sea was spent working in the lamp room with all its seasickness-encouraging smells. However, I survived and discovered that my stomach was as strong as it needed to be. I could throw it as far as anybody else.

Three weeks later I was in Malta with the Mediterranean Fleet which then used the island with its fully efficient dockyard as its base.

Here I was introduced to the Maltese hairdressing profession and that was some experience. Those scissors went everywhere that there was hair to be cut — in the ears, round the eyebrows, up the nose — *snip, snip*. I was glad I was sitting down at the time! Then came the shampoo and the obligatory neck massage with the twisting of the head until it stuck sideways and then had to be twisted back again. It was great for sobering you up after a bellyful of Pharsons Blue beer on a hot afternoon.

After a few weeks on *Maidstone* I was transferred to *H.M.S. Penelope*. This was a warship to delight any schoolboy's dream — a new light cruiser serving her first commission — a sleek, trim, well armed and efficient ship with a good captain and crew. Her ship's company had won most of the fleet awards for both work and sport. Naturally I was proud to be part of that august body. Also, my pay had risen to half-a-crown per day.

With *H.M.S. Penelope* I took part in the 'Spanish patrol' where our duty was to preserve the freedom of the seas during the Civil War so that neutral ships could go about their lawful business and I remember spending the whole night battened down in the ship's forward magazine with racks of cordite for company while we stood between a British cargo ship and one of General Franco's cruisers. We dropped depth charges now and then for training purposes and this did not please Mussolini's 'neutral' submarines. Unfortunately we were not allowed to do anything about the 'neutral' German and Italian planes which flew over us on their way to attack the legitimate Spanish government forces.

We also went to Haifa and landed our Royal Marines to help the British army units who were trying to keep peace between the Jews and Arabs and being hated by both sides for their trouble. There was so much hostility in Palestine that if we went ashore for leave or duty we had to carry a trenching tool handle for our personal protection. We were there in September 1938 when Mr. Chamberlain went to Munich and handed over Czechoslovakia to Germany's good keeping, coming back with a piece of paper signed by a chap called Adolph Hitler. Our Prime Minister believed Adolph — most of us did not.

The Country was partially mobilised for war at that time and within forty-eight hours *Penelope* was at her war station in Port Said fully armed and ready. However, the British government dared not call Hitler's bluff so we just lay at our moorings at the entrance to the Suez Canal watching troopships filled with jeering Italian soldiers on their way to try out their new tanks and poison gas against the Abyssinian tribesmen armed with state of the art spears. The tanks and gas won easily.

The sheltered and well-protected harbour of Port Said was divided into a number of mooring facilities where ships of all nationalities tied up and waited their turn to be guided through the Suez Canal. There *Penelope* lay between two large, modern cargo ships which arrogantly displayed the Nazi Swastika. Their presence caused our old hands to observe that they would be a rare prize for us if war broke out now. We were ready to board them and take possession if and when the order was given.

In 1938 the value of a captured vessel — or 'prize' — would be shared out among the crew of the ship or ships by whom she had been taken and could provide a nice bit of pocket money for the lowly paid sailors. That rule was changed later when those whom even the Admirals must obey decided that it would be fairer to share out the total amount of prize-money between **all** of the Royal Navy personnel as well as those men of the Royal Air Force who had served with Coastal Command.

Since most of the enemy captains were ordered to scuttle their ships as soon as we poked our nose in, there was not a lot of prize money to go around and we finished up with a handout worth little more than a couple of pints and a packet of crisps. Well, every little helps, as the cat said!

While we were in Port Said the entrance to the Canal was very busy from early light and I was always intrigued to watch the many tugboats going out to pick up their towage and piloting responsibilities. I could not help thinking how much they reminded me of dogs and men! The small tugs made a hell of a racket, *pheep, pheep, pheep, yap, yap, yap*, like tormented terriers as they scurried away and came back into port with a poky little freighter about the size of a parochial punt.

The large, ocean-going boats just gave a calm, dignified *waahoof*, like big bull mastiffs as they steamed out of harbour to reappear in charge of a huge liner or a thirty thousand ton battleship.

We were in Malta again in the Spring of 1939 when the fearless Italians invaded poorly armed Albania. It was Sunday evening and I was ashore in Valetta attending an evening service at a Baptist church with other chaps from the fleet. Halfway through the service the preacher announced that all Royal Navy personnel were to return to their ships. As we left, the large congregation of mostly servicemen and their families began singing the hymn 'God be with you till we meet again'. Sadly we did not meet again. The fleet departed next morning for Alexandria and was no longer based at Malta.

In the summer of 1939 *Penelope* was suddenly ordered home to pay off and recommission. I had expected to be left behind since I had not served the required two-and-a-half years on the station but I was told I should be staying as one of the new complement, which suited me just fine. I felt as if I were a part of that ship. I was granted two weeks' leave.

Before going on furlough I bought myself some civvies from one of the big stores in Portsmouth. I got a sports jacket, trousers, shirt, necktie and a pair of shoes and I had change out of two pounds of British money. When I reached home I found that most of my age group had been called up with the volunteer reserves or the new 'militia' so I was on my own. However, halfway through my leave I was recalled to the ship where I was told to pack my bag and take myself off to Portsmouth barracks. That would not be the only time I would get a 'leave cancelled' telegram. I was disappointed, but I should have known it would be too good to last.

The holiday I had been forced to give up was wasted hanging around Portsmouth depot doing little except fall in, fall out, salute, and watch a lot of recalled pensioners reporting for duty, some of them in wheelchairs or on crutches. I was informed that I should be joining my next ship as a leading hand. Promotion had come much sooner than I had expected. It was only a small step up a very tall ladder but the new responsibility was worth an extra ninepence per day which was enough to pay for two pints of N.A.A.F.I. beer, if you cared for that sort of thing. I was then given a medical and dental examination and an X-ray. I also received a draft chit to another light cruiser named *H.M.S. Coventry*.

And so on the 23rd August 1939, still full of the old Rule Britannia and all the rest of it I picked up my kitbag and hammock and my green reinforced fibre R.N. issue suitcase and joined the transport to Southslip jetty in Portsmouth dockyard and there it was — a naval architect's nightmare, a 'Gash Boat' if ever I saw one!

What had once been a smart little ship of the line looked as if it had been vandalised by a Heath Robinson 'on something'. There were small guns sticking up all over the deck looking as if they might have been dropped from on high. For a fighting top above the bridge was what looked like a giant roasting tin which appeared to be balanced precariously on top of the foremast. A big rangefinder control tower was stuck above this contraption. In the name of Harry Tait's navy, what kind of a war was that meant to fight? I would find out soon enough — the hard way.

She was one of six 'C' class cruisers brought into service during the second half of the Great War. Between 1935 and 1939 they were converted to defence ships whose main function was to protect the other ships of the fleet as well as the merchant ships on convoy against attack by enemy aircraft. But their Lordships did not want to spend very much money on them. Our main armament was ten four-inch calibre high angle, quick-firing guns of last war vintage plus an eight barrel two-pounder pom-pom capable of firing a thousand rounds per minute. Also there were several small machine-guns which proved to be useless. She was equipped with two rangefinder directors and the huge tin box was the air defence observation platform (A.D.O.P.) with eight lookout positions. Needless to say, all this extra weight made her uncomfortable in a rough sea.

For all the modernisation she was still an old ship, as I came to learn especially in my early days aboard when one of my duties was that of lamp trimmer. There were no fancy tanks in which to store the sperm oil. Here it was kept in huge barrels and had to be siphoned into the hand can by the simple process of sucking through a rubber tube and letting it go at the correct moment. Very often, there would be a sudden heave at the wrong time and for the next few days everything I ate or drank tasted of paraffin.

When I came to the ship she was taking on board what was to be her war complement. Many of the 'regular' servicemen were replaced by reservists. A division from the London Royal Naval Volunteer Reserve (R.N.V.R.) had arrived a few days earlier for their annual training and suddenly found themselves mobilised. They had been sent on forty-eight hours' leave to get their affairs in order. Now joining the ship were R.N.V.R. ratings from other divisions like Clyde, Tyne, and Mersey along with Royal Naval Reserves (R.N.R.) men who normally earned their living in the Merchant Navy or fishing fleet.

The most experienced men were from the Royal Fleet Reserve (R.F.R) who had served up to twenty-five years before being discharged to pension which tied them to the Service for the rest of their lives. Some were over sixty years old, real 'ancient mariners', and a few had served with the renowned Dover Patrol under Commander Evans of the 'Broke'. All wore medal ribbons from the last war and it was a pity they could not have been spared a second ordeal which many of them did not survive.

We felt sorry for them but we had to admit that when the first shots were fired these old-timers provided the backbone that we green youngsters needed. Mind you, it was not long before we were all veterans ourselves.

There were some great characters among the reservists like 'Old Tom' who had lost his sense of taste and smell and could eat anything remotely digestible, often turning a few weaker stomachs in the process. There was a fun loving old stoker we called 'Ginger' who was given to profound rejoinders like, 'Hang the expense, give the cat a canary' or, if somebody remarked that it was cold he would say, 'Pull your shirt over it'. He said when he went to his first ship the chief stoker asked him, 'What do you want — an easy five minutes or a rough half-hour?' He took the rough half-hour — at first. He smoked a small old-fashioned clay pipe and tried to persuade me to smoke the same but I just did not have the stomach. He taught me how to roll the leaf tobacco.

Some of the crew were good athletes, artistes, musicians and all sorts of talents. There were sincere churchgoers as well as the 'Bible bashers' and a few atheists. Of course, in a company of four hundred men, there were bound to be a few homosexuals — normally referred to as 'brown hatters' or 'rear admirals' but these chaps kept their private thoughts and feelings to themselves. Anybody found guilty of 'an act of sodomy with man or beast', as it was written in the articles of war posted up in every ship, was liable to dismissal from the Service and a sentence of two years in prison, so most sailors played the part of the three wise monkeys and neither saw, heard nor spoke about it except to treat it all as a bit of a joke. In any case the young ratings always looked upon the old 'stripeys' with a certain amount of suspicion although their intentions were most likely quite honourable. A lot of youngsters were happy to listen to and learn from the old hands until they were teased with stories about 'Daddies and Wingers'. It was noticed that the older men who were that way inclined preferred the pleasure of young boys. One time when transporting an Army pipe band the pipe major was heard to advise the young drummers, 'Keep awa' fae they sailors or they'll snatch yer hoops'.

It could be a serious matter if there were an involvement between junior and senior ratings and even more so between officers and men. There was a wise old parody, 'The hand that wanks the coxswain rules the boat' and there was talk about 'vicious circles' which, I think, had something to do with false teeth! I never did get to see that golden rivet!

When I first joined the navy I was wisely advised that I should never argue about politics, religion or sport so I kept my opinions to myself.

Part of the ship's complement were eight supply ratings comprising a chief petty officer, 2 petty officers, 2 leading hands and 3 supply assistants. The two petty officers were well past their sell-by date and were drafted to a shore base after a few months of the war. Pete and I, as leading hands, replaced them, and young recruits joined us to make up the numbers. We were all promoted to petty officer by the time we left the ship. Charlie, in his late thirties, was a good supply chief, widely experienced but young at heart. He gave us youngsters plenty of encouragement and we knew that we should always have his full backing whenever it was needed. In the main we were a lucky lot of lads and happy in our work.

That was the ship's company in late August 1939 — a ditty box of ordinary decent men aged between seventeen and seventy from all parts of the British Isles and Ireland. An assorted kitbag of Jolly Jacks with no particular claim to fame or fortune — drooling over Deanna Durbin or lusting after Lena Horne and bubbling over Bing Crosby. Louis Armstrong was a favourite too.

On 25th August 1939, now fully mobilised we headed for Gibraltar to join the Mediterranean Fleet, drilling and exercising all the way. During a brief stop at 'The Rock' we cleared lower deck and the Captain told us we were bound for Alexandria where we should wait to see what was going to happen. It was possible that we might become involved in a large-scale hostility but he would let us know when somebody told him about it.

Then followed the usual lecture by the medical officer about the pitfalls awaiting young men in foreign ports and certain dangerous liaisons between sailors and designing persons of the opposite sex whose main purpose in life was to ensnare them with their spellbinding and wicked charms. The sick berth petty officer translated the good man's wise words into English which the young ratings more easily understood, not that they paid any attention to his advice, as was proved later by the number of patients in 'Rose Cottage' confirming the opinion of the old timers that 'it will draw you further than gunpowder will blow you'.

After a few hours in Gibraltar we moved on to Malta and then to Alexandria where the large Mediterranean Fleet was in harbour. We arrived there during the afternoon and moored alongside the outer mole at the harbour entrance for the night. The next morning was Sunday, September 3rd 1939. We carried out the normal morning duties — clean and tidy up ship, divisions etc. We did not have a chaplain so there were no morning prayers. In peacetime, this was the day that only essential work was done and most of us took it easy. Usually there would be shore leave in the afternoon. The routine call would be 'Hands to make and mend clothes'.

At stand easy, enjoying our usual 'cuppa' we listened to the wireless while Mr. Chamberlain regretted that Mr. Hitler had not played the game. He refused to take his 'liberating forces' out of Poland so that now we found ourselves at war with the beastly Germans and how he had been let down by the man who gave his word and what a sad day it was for him, and other such melancholia. We then waited until we were told officially. We had no tannoy or public address system which meant that all orders or messages were passed by word of mouth throughout the ship. This entailed a lot of walking and whistling by the boatswain's mate. It was his usual practice to keep items of less importance until later on so that several of these could be piped with other news at the same time. On this occasion he waited until it was time for the routine order calling the hands from each mess to collect their daily issue of potatoes. He then walked fore and aft piping and calling down each hatch, 'England has declared war on Germany' *whistle* 'Hands to the mess for spuds'.

Of course there then followed the usual discussion as to whether the Scottish, Welsh and Irish ratings were meant to be involved or should it be left to the English alone? And did we have enough spuds to fight them with?

We heard this announcement with mixed feelings. To the young it was an adventure, the reason for which we had joined the navy in the first place. There would be plenty of excitement, maybe a bit of danger, medals to be won and all the girls would be dazzled by the glamour of our uniform and just melt into our arms and so forth.

Anyway, we would soon sort out the Huns. Did we not have the biggest and best fleet in the world? It would be over by Christmas. That's what we thought. The old hands who had seen it all before ventured to suggest that they said the same thing in 1914, but we paid no attention to them. It would be different this time! We knew it all, poor deluded souls that we were.

It had not occurred to us that we might face a lot of disaster, grief and despair. It's funny how you never think of death until it slaps you in the face. Boysaboys — didn't we have a lot to learn!

We spent a few weeks in and around Alexandria, going to sea most days for exercise and training and learning how to fight an enemy who we were sure would be a pushover. It was fine and lightsome under the warm blue sky but then their Lordships decided that there would be no hostilities out here and it was time for us to get back to doing what we were paid for.

By the middle of October we were back in Portsmouth after an uneventful passage except for a challenge off the North African coast by a French destroyer who thought we were an enemy ship and we flashed the correct code of fighting lights only just in time. We also had a U-boat scare in the Bay of Biscay but we pressed on regardless.

We passed a few days in Portsmouth making some alterations including the removal of two of the four-inch guns which had proved to be more of a menace than an asset. We also managed to paint the ship's side under the critical eye of our Captain's young and beautiful wife who hurriedly left the scene when she saw 'Old Tom' pretending to enjoy eating something which did not look very appetising or wholesome having been found floating in the water near the gash chute!

That proved to be the very last time the ship was to visit her home port and a week later we were on North Sea patrol and escort duties with our sister ships *H.M.S. Calcutta* and *Cairo*, both now converted to anti-aircraft ships, and more modern than we were. We operated from the Humber estuary where we came to grips with our first assailant in the shape of a Heinkel bomber who seemed to be much more experienced than our lot but he did not linger when we opened up with enough flak to sink the whole German air force. We missed — of course!

From the Humber we patrolled north and south escorting freighters, checking on neutral shipping, and trying to stop supplies getting to Germany. We also kept a lookout for enemy aircraft laying mines all along the east and north-east coasts. During one convoy through the North Sea we were joined by a cargo ship proudly wearing the ensign of Estonia which country had recently been 'liberated' by Stalin as part of his infamous pact with Hitler. I heard one chap remark, 'Another poor sod with no home to go to. Bastard dictators!'

The ship's main engines started to give trouble again and we had to go into dry dock at Immingham, port of call for the fishing town of Grimsby. Like most of the same class of ship, this one was ready for the scrapyard. The repairs were estimated to take three weeks so we were given six days' leave each watch.

Grimsby was a great little town. The folk were very kind and they made the sailors welcome. Many colourful stories have been told about nights ashore in that town and there may be many tales yet to tell but we did not have much time there to enjoy the place. We left one of our supply ratings in a Grimsby hospital. He was treated very well until he took a turn for the nurse. They were caught in a cupboard doing their best for Britain.

In mid-November, still only half repaired, we were ordered to make our best speed for the Shetland Islands and Sullom Voe which was being paid too much attention by the German air force.

It was a wild journey with the wind becoming stronger and the sea more angry by the minute. She was not a good sea boat at the best of times with a severe dip, roll and shake and a nasty habit of flooding the forecastle and the forward mess decks. It was not much fun having to drop from a damp hammock in the early hours to gather up what you could salvage of food and mess equipment from the deck while trying to bale out the ankle deep water and other unpleasantries before you could set to and prepare breakfast then carry on with the normal daily routine.

As we came up by the Pentland Firth the wind was gusting to storm force ten and the sea was running very high. Lifelines were rigged along the upper deck and it was not safe to move without hanging on to them. Sometimes we thought we could easily turn right over and the gun crews had to find shelter wherever they could and hang on for dear life. We still had a long way to go and there was no sign of the storm abating but we had to keep going.

We took it for granted that our good Captain who was an experienced seaman knew where we were but most of the ship's company had no idea, except that we were somewhere on the west side of the Shetland Islands — wherever they were. All I knew was that there were an awful lot of rocks and cliffs and we seemed to be uncomfortably close to them with a storm force wind blowing us closer still.

Somewhere north of Ronas Voe our steering mechanism gave up the ghost and we came to a sudden stop. We had lost control of the rudder and with the wind pushing us towards the shore it began to look as if this four-and-a-half thousand tons of steel was in danger of finding the last resting place for four hundred men.

With a magnificent effort the emergency party scrambled and clawed their way to the stern of the ship where they squeezed through the narrow hatch into the crammed space of the tiller flat below. There they had to unship the heavy steel rudder and connect it to the capstan which they heaved and turned by hand — a test of courage, strength and endurance about which most of us were completely unaware at the time. Meanwhile, those men with no vital duty to do below were on the upper deck wearing a life-jacket — if they could get hold of one — just staring at the rocks as they came closer and closer as if they were determined to tear us to pieces. It seemed that the tiller crew managed to heave the rudder and steady the old ship just at the very last minute and, daft though it was when we thought about it afterwards, hands reached out as if we hoped to push the huge vessel away from the dreaded reef.

Eventually the guts of the steering party and the skilled seamanship of the Captain brought the ship around the point and down into Yell Sound and the shelter of Colla Firth where we anchored and carried out repairs during the afternoon and evening. We considered ourselves very lucky to be alive. A lonely Dornier bomber flew around to see what was going on but he did not come too close and a few bursts from our four-inch guns made him less inquisitive.

The heads and the wash places were quite busy that night before we turned in!

Next morning with our steering gear temporarily under control and the weather a little less hostile we ventured south through Yell Sound to anchor in the north of Sullom Voe where we relieved the light cruiser *H.M.S. Cardiff* as guard ship looking after the oil tanker *War Divan*, also a flotilla of Sunderland and London flying boats with their supply and accommodation ship *Manilla*. These flying boats had a very important duty patrolling the North Sea as far as the Norwegian coastline looking for enemy submarines and surface vessels. Being undefended and so vulnerable they were an obvious target for the enemy bombers.

We began to feel like a mother hen taking them under our wings.

There were no shore based anti-aircraft guns anywhere near Sullom Voe when we arrived and the only air defence in Shetland appeared to be three old Gloucester Gladiator biplanes based at Sumburgh on the southern tip of the islands. Keen and brave though they were, with their limited range and speed they usually arrived too late to catch the enemy.

H.M.S. Cardiff was oiled up and ready to leave when we arrived a day later than scheduled. She was an old six-inch gun cruiser of the same class as ourselves but she had not been converted and had to make do with two high angle guns of three-inch calibre and a few old machine-guns for anti-aircraft defence. She had been in action against bombers a few days ago but her only kill had been a couple of rabbits for which foul deed the Luftwaffe had been forced to take the blame.

A London newspaper produced a photograph of a crofter holding aloft the 'victims'. Considering that they were supposed to have been hit by a five-hundred pound bomb, the rabbits looked remarkably well put together. *Cardiff* left Sullom Voe to resume her unenviable task of patrolling the North Sea and Atlantic Ocean. The rabbits probably got stuffed or was it the Germans?

Soon after we anchored in Sullom Voe we were looked over by the usual nosey parker patrol plane but he did not hang around after our first barrage and the rest of the day was peaceful. The storm had eased, giving us a chance to do a bit of tidying up and carrying out a few repairs. The upper deck had taken a right hammering on the way north.

We had not yet been fitted with R.D.F., later to become known as radar, so we had to depend on the early warning defence station at Wick and the alertness and eyesight of our own lookouts who, like the gun crews, were at defence stations which meant being on duty for four hours and then four hours off during the daylight hours. When unidentified aircraft were spotted the alarm rattlers shrieked an ear splitting warning and the ship's company closed-up very quickly to full action stations.

Before we left Grimsby I had been 'green' enough to pass an eyesight test and found that I was volunteered for lookout duties in the foretop A.D.O.P. As it turned out I quite liked this job. It was a break from boring office duties and it got me into the fresh air — be it ever so cold. In the early days of the war, duffel coats seemed to be available only to dockyard civil servants but I found that I could keep myself reasonably warm by wearing a borrowed oilskin coat over my raincoat and two pairs of socks inside gumboots. We were not issued with much in the way of warm clothing and most of the winter woollies provided by the good ladies of Great Britain and the Commonwealth only caught up with us when we were serving in a hot climate.

Of course, I still had to keep up with my pen-pushing duties which meant that I did not have much spare time.

I worked with a fine watch, mostly cooks, stewards and supply ratings — day men to give us our official title. There were also three R.N.V.R. ordinary seamen, two from Clyde and one from Mersey, plus a couple of able seamen. They were a great bunch of lads full of wit and humour typical of the carefree youth of those days.

During our four-hour watch, six of us at a time would sit on swivel chairs holding binoculars fixed to adjustable geometric scales so that when he spotted something the lookout could instantly report the target's bearing and elevation with relation to the ship and these details would be shouted out to the other lads with the handsets who would pass them on to the control director above us and the gun crews below. There were two special lookout instruments facing forward manned by a petty officer gunnery instructor and a sergeant Royal Marine. The ship's gunnery officer or the Captain Royal Marines who was also an expert in plane spotting would be on watch with us. It was quite a chummy little party. From above we must have looked like a dish of rampant sausages!

To reach the observation platform we had to climb a vertical ladder from the bridge to the top of the mast then heave ourselves up through a hole in the floor like a disorientated worm looking for a bird. It was easy enough if you were unaffected by vertigo and you could reassure yourself that the ferocious wind would not carry out its threat to tear you away from the ladder and throw you into the raging sea which seemed to be trying to reach up and grab you. 'Just ignore it and it will go away', we were told. When I first started as a lookout it was meant to be just a stopgap and when we went to action stations the trained seamen would take over. This practice caused a right mix-up-in-a-dixie with the men tearing down the mast meeting those coming up and getting in each other's way, so that the action could be over before some of us reached our required posts. When somebody pointed out to the gunnery officer that this routine drill seemed to be a matter of pure effluence the order was changed and the temporary hands stayed at their spyglasses which made life much more interesting.

We did not realise it at first but on a clear day the crisp, pure air around Shetland could have a sort of tranquilising effect on us and we had to watch that we did not doze off when there was not much activity. To keep ourselves awake we would make up songs and rhymes — clean words of course — about topical subjects like things we saw and heard, and we would voice our observations about the goings on in the heather or the snow as we swept the hills with our Barr and Stroud long-range opera glasses.

There was an old croft on the nearby hillside whose sole occupants appeared to be an elderly couple with a cat and a cow and some hens. During the milder days of late autumn and early winter sometimes the ship would swing quite close in and we would have a clear view of the croft house. I did not know if the old lady could see the colour of our warning signal flags but she always seemed to sense if there was danger. Every morning at about ten o'clock she would open the door and look at the sky. If the weather looked reasonable she would start working around the house and feed a few hens which appeared from nowhere. Then she went next door and came out with a cow which she tethered on the bit of grassland near the house. After that was done she went back inside the house to bring out an elderly fellow whom she sat on a chair beside the front door. When her companion was settled she carried on with her work on the bit of cultivated land which seemed to be cropped with cabbages and potatoes. If we flew the yellow warning, meaning possible danger from aircraft, she would take the old chap inside. If we flew the red warning and ran to action stations — perhaps she heard the alarm rattlers — she also took the cow indoors then went back into the house and shut the door and windows. When it was all clear she would repeat the performance — first the cow, then the old man and on with the show. Sometimes, when the weather was poor the folks might not appear for several days and the lads would start to worry, but there was not much we could do about it as we were supposed to be looking out for enemy aircraft and not friendly crofters. We just hoped they were all right.

The first few days of our sojourn at Sullom Voe brought several nosey Heinkels or Dorniers for a snoop around but they seemed to be only checking and kept out of range. Then one day, having 'cased the joint' the Luftwaffe surely decided that it was time to come in and clean up the property, and they meant business!

It was an ideal day for a surprise attack but we had received early warning from Wick and we were ready. We knew exactly where they would come, through the gap in the hills to the north-west. We had been told to expect a large attacking force and we were waiting. We could not see them but we could almost feel their breath as they came closer and closer. Every gun was bearing and ready to fire. The trainers and layers had the correct direction and the fuses were properly set, the rangefinder had been measuring up those hills ever since we came here. It would be impossible to miss.

'Come on you square headed b******s, come on you horrible Huns. Steady lads, wait till you see the whites of their eyes, steady, ste-a-d-y.' Then the control officer panicked and pressed the trigger just a couple of minutes too soon and a massive barrage filled the sky with flak just far enough ahead of them for the bombers to take evasive action. What should have been a resounding victory and great propaganda turned out to be a stupendous failure.

We did, however, pick up a few distress calls and our fire-power obviously impressed those who depended on our protection. They were quick to signal their appreciation and late in the afternoon the Royal Air Force personnel sent over a pinnace with an invitation to share their meagre hospitality on board *Manilla* where a glass of beer went down very nicely with the lucky few who were able to go.

The weather worsened again the next day and we were lashed with gale force winds for a week or more. It became necessary to keep up a head of steam as well as anchors bow and stern. It certainly knows how to blow in this part of the world. In the A.D.O.P. it was cold and wet, but we kept our end up by making up rumours and wagering how long it would be before somebody came to tell us confidentially about the latest secret he had just heard, which would be the same story we had started.

The weather was too poor to expect much enemy aircraft activity and even our own flying boats were unable to take off very often. When they did go out on patrol it was a very difficult and hazardous task bringing them back to their moorings. They were frequently in action with enemy fighter planes and came back with dead and wounded among their crew. It was not an easy life for the airmen. It required a lot of courage and dedication.

Our life here in storm lashed Sullom Voe was a picnic compared with that of the sailors on the Northern Patrol, as we could see from the state of the ships which limped into the Voe for fuel and provisions. They sometimes came alongside so that our engineers could help with urgent repairs. On one of these occasions we had a new Tribal class destroyer alongside with a problem in the engine room which our highly skilled artisans could not locate. A young Clyde R.N.V.R. ordinary seaman named Jimmy told me he had helped to build the ship whilst serving his apprenticeship. I passed this information on to the chief engineroom artificer who took 'Wee Jimmy' down below where they found the trouble and fixed it.

When told, our senior engineer agreed that it was stupid for a skilled man to be wasting his time as an ordinary seaman and pushed his name through for transfer to Engineroom branch. It took more than a year for the paperwork to be completed before 'Wee Jimmy' was able to use his skills where they were most needed. The Royal Navy was desperately short of engineers at that time.

Still it was only a 'phoney war' — wasn't it?

Once in a while I had to go across to the oiler *War Divan* with fresh provisions, including bread for the smaller ships such as armed trawlers and minesweepers. They could not carry much in the way of stores and provisions but were required to spend long periods at sea. It was usually choppy so that I was apprehensive enough about the trip across, but coming back in the darkening afternoon was an adventure to which I definitely did not look forward. Instead of bringing the boat alongside the gangway the coxswain went straight to the port boom. I was then left to climb up a swinging Jacob's ladder and edge precariously along a round wooden pole which, to me, seemed to be about two inches in diameter although it would probably have been much thicker, then I had to climb up a straight, narrow iron ladder and scramble over the side onto the deck.

The boat's crew who were doing this all the time thought nothing of it. I did not think much of it myself!

The beginning of December saw the weather ease and we were allowed ashore, just a few of us at a time, to stretch our legs and kick a football around for a couple of hours on a patch of grassland nearby. We could not stray far from the pier in case we had to make a quick dash back to the ship if danger threatened. We could only go ashore if it was damp and the sky overcast so it soon lost its attraction.

There were three lucky men who landed every day when the weather was reasonable and the sea calm enough for the motor cutter. They were 'Sticks' the ship's postman, Alf the canteen manager, and Sam the chief wardroom steward. They went after breakfast to the jetty at Sullom and then by hired car to the town of Lerwick. The Paymaster Commander also went into town quite frequently on business known only to himself. We had a signalman lodged ashore at Sullom. He had a telephone connection to the Naval Base in Lerwick which had been set up in the town's old fish market offices and he would take or pass messages to the ship by Aldis signal lamp.

Around this time our thoughtful Captain made arrangements for the provision of a canteen on the pier at Sullom. A local contractor put up the building and we sent a shipwright and his mate — a R.N.V.R. able seaman — ashore whenever possible to build the bar and furnishings and lay a wooden floor. Unfortunately for some, the beer arrived before the work was finished and from then on they laid about one floorboard per day! In another act of benevolence we had been allocated the use of a former fishing drifter as a tender so it was easier for the not altogether sober carpenters to get back aboard the ship!

It was now possible for a leave party to go ashore for a drink. It was usually a fairly rough trip, getting on and off the drifter in darkness and risking life and limb in the process. I did not avail myself of this masochistic pleasure. I thought it was a long way to go for a pint.

Then the good Captain waxed even more liberal and arranged with a local firm to provide a small motor coach to take a party for a few hours' night leave into the town of Lerwick. The coach could carry only thirty-two passengers and some men from the *Manilla* and *War Divan* were included in that number, so our group was limited to twenty men and you had to wait your turn. The weather needed to be favourable and the roads clear. Then we suffered the hazardous crossing from the ship to Sullom pier from where we crammed into a blacked out bus for the long journey over the narrow single track road into Lerwick. The bus left the town at half-past-ten and the return journey was even more of an endurance test.

I still thought it was a long way to go for a pint! I was content to stay aboard — or so I told myself. I had no way of knowing at this time that the moving finger which chronicles the story of my life had already started to write a chapter which will not end until I finally cross the bar.

And it started with nothing more auspicious than a few dead sheep!

The ship's Paymaster Commander at the start of the war was a gentleman who hailed from the Channel Islands. He was a good boss to us although some of the men thought him a little eccentric. During action stations he wore a handmade quilted jacket, designed to keep a body afloat as well as warm, and he used to stuff all the paper money from the ship's safe into his pockets — presumably if the worst came to the worst he could always take it with him!

Whilst on one of his frequent visits to the R.N. Headquarters in Lerwick he took it upon himself to order a regular supply of fresh meat from a local purveyor, probably at a fraternal gathering or something similar. The result was that two or three times a week the ship's tender would arrive alongside loaded to the gunwales with huge carcasses of mutton. The working party seamen who had to carry them down below would swear they were Shetland ponies until an old hand put them at their ease with the remark, 'Horses don't stink like that!'

The ratings started to grumble when their daily ration was never anything but mutton with not a taste of beef or pork. It was no good their complaining to the ship's butcher because he hardly noticed the carcasses hanging up like Christmas decorations around his lordly domain. Since I was the Jack Dusty I had to take the blame for this peculiar skullduggery and the lads started making rude sheep noises at me whenever I passed by.

The ship's butcher — I never knew him under any other name than 'Butch' — was a Royal Marine who had managed to trundle his way through life in a state of permanent alcohol-assisted unawareness. He was responsible for storing, preparing, serving out, and recording the issue of all the mess decks' allocation of fresh meat and vegetables. He also helped with the daily issue of grog!

We could make nothing of such records as he kept; some messes would get too much while others were issued short. I don't think he ever looked at the weighing scales. If anybody questioned him he would pay no attention at first and then suddenly frighten the life out of you with a sharp, 'What's up, what's up?' You were happier if he did not have a meat cleaver in his hand at the time. When he realised he was being spoken to he would raise his right forefinger in salute and answer, 'So there you are, there you are' and then ignore you completely. The stock figures were always wrong and we could have done with a whole tumble of acrobats to balance the books. Whenever the old supply petty officer ventured to tackle him about the stock he would say, 'Ah well, yes then, I was just coming to tell you about it. I saw another dirty great rat in the beefscreen this morning'.

Lucky old 'Butch'. He left the ship a few months later. About four years on I met him one night walking along the street in Portsmouth. I said hello and 'Butch' raised his forefinger in salute, answered my greeting with a polite, 'So there you are, there you are' and walked on by. I never saw him again.

My immediate boss, the supply petty officer in charge of victualling, was an elderly chap who had been a ship's steward in the Royal Navy in the days before the Battle of Jutland and had gone to pension about fifteen years ago, before being recalled in August 1939. He always insisted on being in charge of the rum issue and he was about a hundred 'proof' himself. Whenever he went to report to the 'old man' he would first chew a handful of dry tea leaves 'to keep the breath sweet, old dear' as he would say. He was a kindly old soul but definitely away with it. He called everybody 'old dear' and wanted to be referred to as Mr. Green.

One day he told me to prepare for a load of fresh mutton coming on board tomorrow and he was taken aback when, speaking with all the best of diplomacy and deference I could muster, I asked him, politely, where the hell was I going to store the unmentionable ovine. It was only then that he began to realise that all things were not bright and beautiful — nor even wise and wonderful. So, after another self-offering of the unbrewed beverage, he plodded off to see the 'old man' to find out what was to be done.

It was decided that I should be sent into Lerwick to see the mutton merchant and sort out the 'mistake'. The Paymaster could not go to see him himself for reasons of discretion, probably something to do with an ageing grandmother! Since I was due to keep the forenoon watch on the A.D.O.P. on the morrow it meant that arrangements had to be made for my replacement and as those in authority hated having to rearrange anything a suitable explanation had to be invented. As expected, later that day the Paymaster Commander got in touch with his Lerwick agent and sorted out the problem but it was decided that he would lose face in the wardroom, especially with the Gunnery Officer, if I turned up for duty as usual in the forenoon.

To keep up appearances I was sent on the duty boat next morning to the R.N. supply office in Lerwick with an unimportant message which could quite easily have been delivered by the ship's postman.

In the town, I had to hang around all day until the duty run back in the afternoon. I arranged to meet up with Sam, 'Sticks' and Alf at midday in a well patronised restaurant known as 'Henry's Café' situated at the foot of a very steep street named Bank Lane. There I should be able to spend the meal voucher I had collected valued at one shilling and sixpence.

I idled away the forenoon strolling around the small picturesque town with its narrow paved street and small busy shopping centre. The island's main business seemed to be done here and the small shops were all clean and tidy. Most of the shop assistants were ladies and the bosses appeared to be long past their prime.

I had very little money to spend but it was pleasant to wander around and speak to the 'natives'. Like my shipmates I knew very little about the geography, let alone the inhabitants of these far flung islands and, begging pardon for my ignorance, I was delighted to learn that they spoke English and a damned sight better English than did most of us! Mind you, this ignorance was not restricted to those of us from south of the Border. About a dozen years later I spoke to a Glaswegian school teacher and she told us in all innocence that she had always believed the Shetlands to be just 'a rock with sheep on it'.

It was easy to see that the Shetland folk were a sturdy, intelligent and very kindly people who seemed to dislike being called Scottish or any other appellation than Shetlander. They had a natural sympathy for anybody who was — as the older folk said, 'a poor fanting bugger fae da Sooth' whatever that was meant to be. Most Shetlanders earned their living from the sea so there was an affinity with all sailors.

I could not help noticing the beauty of the local ladies. Old or young they all seemed extremely attractive with bonny, unpainted complexions and smart individual hairstyles. They all wore quietly colourful clothes with a lot of fine knitwear. Most of all they had that lovely smile which looked so warm and friendly. I am sure that I have never seen so many good looking lasses in any one place. I cannot recall seeing any woman who was ill-favoured. It must be something in the air!

There were not many local men around except those in the older age group. Many of the young and middle-aged, even elderly men, were at sea with ships of the Merchant Fleet or the Royal Navy — mainly minesweepers and even at this early stage of the war there were a few new widows and grieving mothers.

Quite a number of the men, being volunteers in the Territorial Army, were now with the Highland Division and I met a recruiting sergeant, splendidly attired in the uniform of a Gordon Highlander and sporting a ferocious looking waxed moustache, which had a wingspan of at least six inches, and seemed to spread from ear to the 'ereafter! He introduced me to a Lerwick bar which was surely the quaintest pub I had ever seen. It seemed to be in the cellar at the back of a grocer's shop. There were no tables or counter but all the men stood around with a glass of whisky or rum in one hand, and a large screwtop bottle of beer in the other. For the call of nature there was a drain in one corner of the floor with a dripping water tap above. Not surprisingly, there were no lady drinkers there!

In later years I discovered that the town was officially 'dry'. There were no licensed drinking places or public houses and it was illegal to retail short drinks or pints for consumption on the premises. The licensed grocers could wholesale beers, wines and spirits only in bulk. This of course was a great advantage to the local owners of the drinking dens because, being outlawed, they could charge whatever they liked and did very nicely, thank you. They usually had plenty of warning before the routine raid by the excise men or the police.

The more genteel folks, worthy burghers and other such teetotals did their drinking in the posh restaurants where they enjoyed their illicit liquor out of china tea cups in a room set aside for that purpose, which, of course, nobody was supposed to know about. The lurid details of this classless society I learned a few years later. At the time I just assumed it was their way of doing things and no concern of mine. From the point of view of profits it certainly kept down the overheads.

I did not see much in the way of bed and breakfast accommodation but there was one respectable boarding house where a bonnie young chambermaid was reputed to put her knickers under the pillow of any lodger she might fancy!

At about noon I joined up with the lads in Henry's Café and there Sam introduced me to a young waitress with the lovely name of Lilian. She was the prettiest girl I have ever seen to this day and naturally I fell in love straight away. We did not have much time to speak to each other then but I did manage to persuade her to agree that she would go to the pictures with me the next time I was in town. I think neither of us expected to meet again, but as the poet said, 'Love will find a way'.

A few days later I saw the medical officer and complained of toothache. He sent me into Lerwick to see a local dentist who drilled and filled a perfectly sound tooth at His Majesty's expense, just so Lilian and I could have our promised visit to the North Star cinema where we held hands and watched a film called 'The Great Waltz' which I had already seen three times.

After that I took every available opportunity of a run ashore to see my heart's desire and I was overjoyed to spend the evening of Christmas Day 1939 at her home, where I met some of the most wonderful people I have ever known.

Ah, those halcyon days, few though they were. How we enjoyed the brief hours together — joining with a bunch of youngsters in snow fighting and sledging down streets and lanes with gay abandon — watching the surf breaking gently over small, romantic moonlit beaches — clinging closely together as we strolled along the snow covered lane by the lonely, unoccupied herring stations on a clear starry night in January and being challenged by army sentries, who seemed to have not very much idea of what they were supposed to do or why they were there at all. They never shot at us so they were probably in a hurry to get back to their card game in the dug-out. Maybe they had no ammunition for their rifles!

I suppose it would all seem so simple minded and 'gooey' to the sophisticates of later generations, but it was before the world went mad and we were young, shy and very much in love. We could still believe in things in those days before disillusionment set in. Where did they go? And why? The world seemed to change so much in later years. I suppose we were lucky to have lived our young lives when we did. We were so 'innocent' and there was much to look forward to. We still had chivalry, with honour and respect.

There was not a lot to do aboard the ship at night. We had no cinema or library but there was a very small recreation room where ratings were permitted to smoke. It was rather uncomfortable but at that time we were not allowed to light up on the mess deck and you could hardly enjoy a 'drag' on the upper deck in the black-out, when no lights at all must be seen. As winter closed in the nights became longer and we had up to eighteen hours of darkness out of the twenty-four. There were no city lights in Sullom Voe then.

There was nowhere to go but the darkened mess decks except for those fortunate enough to have offices or workshops and they were likely to have a lot of visitors looking for asylum. The men thought up various ways of passing the time and one fad which developed particularly among the young men of the London R.N.V.R. was the sport of growing beards — or trying to. Some did not have the face for it.

It was the general order of things in the Royal Navy that men must have their hair cut short and be clean shaven at all times. You were not allowed to have sideburns and definitely not a moustache, unless you were a Royal Marine. Beards were frowned upon by most commanding officers and if you wished to grow a 'set' you were obliged to go through the laborious channels of a request to see the Captain through the First Lieutenant, through your Divisional Officer etc etc for permission to 'discontinue shaving'. When granted this favour the beards had to be kept trimmed and neat in accordance with the King's Rules and Admiralty Instructions (K.R.A.I.) which cited as an example the bearded sailor on a packet of Players cigarettes with the ship's name *Hero* on his cap ribbon.

Once they started to grow, you had to keep the whiskers for at least three months. When you wanted to rid yourself of what your mates would tell you was 'like a rat looking through a bunch of oakum' or even less complimentary descriptions you once again had to suffer the long procedure to ask the Captain's permission to 'resume shaving'. When the buzz went around that we might be given home leave very soon all the hairy apes pleaded to be allowed to shave off and were not very happy when the Captain told them they would have to wait until the statutory three months was over. Their lovely young wives or sweethearts would just have to put up with the company of scruffy old men and serve them right I should not wonder.

Some men also started smoking pipes and it was quite amusing to watch them absent-mindedly throw their brand new briars over the side when they went out. Some even tried smoking the real pure leaf tobacco for which they required the advice and assistance of their older and more experienced shipmates.

We could purchase the main brands of tailor-made cigarettes and pipe tobacco at duty free prices from the ship's N.A.A.F.I. canteen if we could get to the hatch while it was open, which did not always suit the time you were off watch. We were also entitled to a monthly ration of duty free tobacco from the 'Pusser's Stores' which was sold at a very cheap rate — whether we were afloat or ashore. We had the choice of a one pound tin of shag which no self-respecting pipe puffer would use, or a pound tin of good quality Virginia cigarette tobacco for rolling your own 'ticklers' which was used by most smokers. The best bargain for a pipe lover was one pound of pure loose leaf, costing only one shilling and sixpence for the monthly ration. This was only for the dedicated and was beloved by most of the older seamen. It had to be made up into a hard compressed roll called a 'perique' so named after the French matelot's pigtail hairstyle.

British sailors never seemed to be able to manage the French pronunciation of 'perique' and used a shorter version of the word, unless there were ladies present.

Rolling a perique of tobacco was a fine art which I never mastered all the time I was in the navy but to the old sailors it was a simple task although always well worthy of an appreciative audience. Firstly, the dry tobacco leaves had to be separated and sorted into size being careful not to break them up if they were too dry. Then they would be sprinkled with water and left for an hour or two to become workable; a drop of rum added to the water did no harm to its taste. When it had become suitably damp it was wrapped up in a piece of hessian and secured by twine. Then you had to 'acquire' a length of pencil thick tarred hemp; nobody asked where this hemp came from but the boatswain's department did use rather a lot of the stuff. It was looped over two opposite hammock hooks and bound around the hessian bundle as tightly as possible, starting at the middle and tapering off to each end. You had to sit on the rope to tighten the binding and the heavier your body weight, the firmer and more smoke-worthy the roll.

It was advisable to put a thick cushion over the cordage before you sat on it otherwise you might find yourself feeling rather cut up about it all. The finished perique was a strong tobacco with plenty of tar but I enjoyed it when I first started smoking at the age of twenty-two, a time of life when I should have had more sense.

I started the habit because I got the impression that pipe-smokers always seemed so relaxed and I do think that it helped me at the time. Really, what calmed me down was the deliberate action of scraping out the pipe bowl, slicing and rubbing the tobacco then filling the pipe and lighting up which required several attempts before you got a good head of steam because the tobacco contained no saltpetre or other chemical poison. That was my excuse, anyway. I gave up the silly habit eventually in a belated effort to save what was left of my lungs and eyesight.

In those days we knew nothing of a connection between smoking and cancer or heart disease. I don't suppose we should have paid much attention, anyway. We did not worry too much about tomorrow. For a lot of people it never came so it was wise advice just to make the best of today.

The old salts averred that the success of a life on the ocean wave depended on three vital requisites — rum, bum, and baccy. I do not know how they would get along in the modern navy now that the daily issue of grog has been discontinued and they can no longer purchase their monthly pound of leaf.

The last week of December 1939 was free from enemy attack mainly due to the severe gales and blizzards which lashed Sullom Voe. Unfortunately the same awful weather which kept the bombers away was not very kind to the less robust equipment attached to the guns. The chief ordnance artificer took every opportunity to make repairs which sometimes left the guns not at their most efficient for a time.

I was on the forenoon watch in the A.D.O.P. on New Year's Day 1940 which dawned bright and clear. The hills were covered by a thick layer of snow and the strong low lying sun shining on the white cover tended to dazzle the eyes as well as dull the mind. The lookout sitting next to me — a Geordie-born Fleet Reservist about thirty-five years of age — reported two enemy aircraft approaching. I had thought my own eyesight to be good but it was about a minute before I could see them and then only as specks. This put them at least twenty miles distant yet he claimed he could see their markings and clearly identified them as 'German bastards'. More valuable minutes ticked by before the powerful lenses of the rangefinder picked them up. Minutes later still, suddenly, as if coming out of a deep sleep we heard the startled voice of the control officer exclaim, 'My God, they're Germans!' which caused my fellow lookout to shout, 'Course the poxy things are. They're bloody Dorniers and they're coming in fast!'

The bombers made direct for our stern so that the pom-pom could not engage them and half the main armament was out of action. One plane turned to draw our fire while the other one dived and dropped a stick of bombs so close as to lift the ship's keel clear of the water. How we failed to turn over only Heaven knows, but we came down with such a crash that it put the ship's dynamo out of action and all the lights and power went off. We were thrown all over the place and it was a miracle that nobody went overboard. There were a few sore backs for a long time afterwards, mine included.

After doing a sweep around the hills the bomber came back flying low as if he were giving us the victory salute or taking our name and number. Being without electricity the guns were not much good but some of the crews managed to get off a few shells by hand firing and the pom-pom let off a few slow rounds with the aid of a foot pedal to generate power. They all missed although the plane came so close that I am sure we could have brought it down if we had only had a bucket of spuds handy. The pilot had not seen the Tribal class destroyer tied up on the other side of the oiler and she opened up with her four-point-sevens as the target flew by, but the bomber just waved them a Happy New Year and flew off into the sunset.

Half-an-hour later, after we had got our stomachs back to where they had been before we were so rudely interrupted, temporary power had been restored and the shipwrights and engineers were examining every inch of the ship below decks, I reported the flashing Aldis lamp of our signalman ashore in Sullom. This time his message was seeking instructions on what he should say to an irate crofter who claimed that we had slaughtered four of his favourite sheep and demanded to know who was going to pay for them.

That night, the B.B.C. radio news bulletin gave a brief mention of the incident but scornfully credited the Luftwaffe with causing no damage or casualties except the murder of four unarmed quadrupeds. The next week a wartime propaganda magazine showed on its front page a photograph of one of the Royal Artillery's new mobile three-point-seven-inch calibre anti-aircraft guns bringing down a Heinkel bomber at Sullom Voe — they must have had a hell of a range wherever they were shooting from. Meanwhile I was wondering if I should have to take delivery of another cargo of mutton tomorrow!

Naturally, we had a song about it in the foretop while the ship's cartoonist had a great picture on the seamen's mess-deck. It was a good joke afterwards, but no laughing matter at the time.

The New Year episode had a profound effect on us. There was no doubt about that. We had convinced ourselves that dealing with an airborne attack was a piece of cake. But so far we had experienced only high-level bombing and most of the enemy had kept at a safe enough distance. This was the first time one of them had made a really determined effort and he had come close to finishing us off. It had been a very near thing and made us realise that the German Air Force would have to be treated with a bit more respect. We still had a lot to learn, but it was beginning to get through to us. The war was no longer a game. Once again, we were lucky to be alive, and Christmas had come and gone.

For most of the time that we had been anchored in Sullom Voe we had been entertained by two seals which spent the day swimming around the ship just staring up at us with their large appealing eyes and accepting all kinds of tit-bits we threw down to them. We had no idea what sex they were — even a lookout's eyesight was not as good as that — but we christened them Sammy and Bessie. After the New Year's Day fiasco they seemed to have gone away and we were concerned they might have been casualties. However, a week later they turned up again to a great cheer from the lads on deck.

During January 1940 we had fairly regular visits from enemy bombers, mostly in flights of two or three, and now and then just a lonely Dornier snooping around. We put up plenty of flak which was good training for the gun crews but the Germans did not seem very keen to press home their attack as if they had lost the stomach for the fight. Perhaps they also had thought it would be over by Christmas.

In late January the Royal Artillery set up a battery of four small anti-aircraft guns and a rangefinder. They did not appear to keep any action watch, and on the first occasion they were called upon to act, only after we had started shooting, they knocked down their rangefinder in the rush and then started putting up flak all over the place mainly in the direction of a R.A.F. Gloucester Gladiator which had come to help.

I don't think the fighter pilot was all that pleased.

I was able to watch the comic opera from my prime seat in A.D.O.P. All it needed was a chorus. It was particularly interesting because we had met some the of 'stars' a few weeks earlier in the N.A.A.F.I. canteen in Lerwick and they had promised that as soon as they became established they would show us how to shoot, 'One shell, one plane', they said.

On February 14th we were relieved by our sister ship *H.M.S. Calcutta* and set forth for England and Chatham dockyard. Most of the ship's company were glad to be moving but I was sad at the thought of the girl I had left behind with not even a chance to say goodbye — and on St. Valentine's of all days.

A lot of water would flow under many bridges before we were to see each other again.

We picked up a small coastal convoy on the way south and the journey was uneventful until we reached the Humber Estuary. There we had to wait while minesweepers used their new-fangled sweeping apparatus to clear a channel through the hundreds of magnetic mines which had been laid all around the east coast while we had been enjoying a rest in the far north.

We crept slowly south, unable to avoid seeing the countless numbers of masts of sunken ships looking like a dense tree plantation in every harbour and estuary. An awesome amount of shipping had been sunk during the last three months. It had to be seen to be believed and I could not help thinking of all the seamen lying below these masts. I had a good view from the foretop and I realised that we could quite easily have been among their number.

Our gunners were well able to drive off the few bombers which came our way but it was a relief when we had crawled through the fog up the shallow, muddy waters of the River Medway to anchor at Sheerness. Next day we went into dry dock to assess the damage done by the near miss at Sullom Voe.

It was my twenty-first birthday which used to be quite an event in those days, but I did not tell my mess mates. I did not feel up to the ritual of 'sippers all round'.

The repairs and renovations were set to take quite some time. The ship had to be fitted with the new degaussing gear to ward off magnetic mines. What a daft world this is — the enemy invents a weapon — we invent a counter to his — he invents a counter to our counter and so on. What a lot of counts we mortals be!

We had to install the new R.D.F. which was invaluable in defence against airborne attack. Metal shields were fitted onto the naked guns to provide some, but not much, protection from shrapnel for the crews. A secondary power generator was installed, an innovation which I personally looked upon as a great blessing. It was automatic emergency lighting which did away with the old oil lamps. What a wonderful thought — no more of that detested task of lamp-trimming which one of the wags opined was 'inclined to get on your wick'.

Two weeks' leave was granted to each watch. Some of the really old hands who went on leave did not come back to the ship and we did not know what became of them. 'Old Tom' was said to have gone sick after eating two fly-papers and a bar of soap. One elderly stoker whose home was only a few miles away came back from leave three weeks adrift and gave the excuse that he had 'missed the train'. A young R.N.R. seaman who came from Banff was several days adrift and his excuse of rail breakdown, fog, enemy action and what-have-you in the far north was accepted by the officer of the day until his photograph appeared in a daily newspaper sitting proudly posing in a Newcastle public house when he was supposed to be held up somewhere far north of the border!

It was decided that our R.N.V.R. gun crews who had been banging away merrily for the past four months should be sent to school so that they could learn all about gunnery and get a little picture of a gun on their sleeve to prove that they were qualified to carry on shooting. This included 'Wee Jimmy' who was still waiting to be transferred to the engineroom artificer branch. The schooling was a bit of a farce because they were instructed by old pensioner chief petty officers who had left the service long ago, having had no modern experience, and who just repeated parrot-fashion from the training manual. If somebody interrupted them they had to go back and start the lecture all over again. Needless to say they were frequently interrupted.

The repairs took much longer than the time estimated — they always did — and it was April before we were fit again to go to sea. We found that we were being prepared for the role of flagship, making us a more important target for attackers. We also had a visit from His Majesty King George VI one wet foggy day when we had to line up for a long time on the jetty alongside the ship. The King, wearing his uniform as Admiral of the Fleet, walked fairly quickly up the ranks, stopping here and there for a chat before passing on to his next Royal duty. He too was a veteran of the Battle of Jutland.

His Majesty seemed more slightly built than I had imagined. He looked quite vulnerable and there was something rather appealing about him. Poor fellow he had a load on his shoulders, but he proved to be well worthy of his office in the grim years ahead. He gave the order to 'Splice the main-brace' and the extra tot of rum was very much appreciated, God bless him!

Before we left Chatham most of the more elderly ratings left the ship and were replaced by younger men who had been called up with the first 'militia' or had volunteered at the beginning of the war.

The supply petty officer 'Old dear' staggered off to greener pastures and I was given his job which I had been doing most of the time anyway. Alf, the N.A.A.F.I manager, was also drafted and he was replaced by an elderly gentleman who became very popular with the ship's company. N.A.A.F.I. personnel were all civilians, not very well paid for their duties, but they still had to endure the discomfort and danger of the ship the same as the rest of us, and this ship could be very uncomfortable in a rough sea, especially when the dockyards kept sticking new bits on the top which did nothing to improve the stability.

Ever since the days of the galley slaves, the men who designed warships, and the Naval powers who controlled them, were never particularly inclined to give much consideration to the home comforts of the men on the lower deck, and living conditions even on a modern ship could scarcely be said to be spacious unless you chanced to be the son of a sardine!

In fact, some of the more nasty minded people among us even ventured the suggestion that we might be a wee bit over-populated.

We now carried a larger complement than the ship had been originally fitted out to accommodate and to make matters worse some of the former messing space had been taken over for other uses and there was nowhere else to live. To those who were sensitive about such things there seemed to be rather too much 'togetherness'. Or something like that!

Men below the rating of petty officer lived in what were grandly referred to as 'broadside messes' and there were up to twenty of these 'homes' to each mess deck. A 'mess' was merely a long wooden table which would be covered by an oilcloth at mealtimes. There was a fitted cupboard and open shelved rack at the end of the table attached to the ship's side and the other end was clear. For seating there was a backless form on each side where you perched cheek to cheek but you could not all sit down at one time. If you leaned backward you came into contact with the chap at the next table, which was great fun if you were both sweating. Overhead were rails or hooks from which you slung your hammock and where you slept head to toe eighteen inches apart from your mess mate. You hoped to goodness his feet would be friendly! Somewhere, not too far away if you were lucky, would be a kit locker where you kept your personal belongings, and there was a small fenced-in space where you stowed your lashed up hammock during the day time.

On and around this mess table you ate your meals, slept, wrote and read your mail, ironed and mended your clothing, cleaned your shoes, played cards or board games, studied for exams, debated or argued, washed up dishes and mess utensils, and prepared your daily meals which you then took up to the ship's galley with your compliments to the cook and the routine request, 'Here you are, chef. Make a mess of this.' — or words less endearing. The cook usually managed to do just that!

The galley crew consisted of a chief petty officer cook, a long serving leading hand, a young regular service trained cook and two young trainees who possessed absolutely no interest and even less ambition to learn the culinary arts. They had been assigned as cooks by those intellectual skivers and con artists on the call-up board because it was considered they were too dumb for anything else, and 'after all surely anybody can be a cook — what does it matter anyway?' The chief cook tried his best with them. He often bought them new rig out of his own pocket because they could not look after their 'whites' but it was to no avail. They hated the job from the start.

It was no use complaining. We grumbled about the breakfast eggs only to be told that they had been boiled for an hour and it was not the cook's fault that they were still hard.

Two pensioner reservists, one a petty officer and the other a leading hand, were appointed to the ship's bakery where with their years of experience they produced an excellent loaf. Oh for some of that bread now!

The bakery was neatly slotted into a small space on the upper deck next to the galley with a door on the port side and a porthole to starboard. If the weather was too fierce for them to open the door, these two jolly old cooks who each measured about sixty inches around the waist would squeeze through the porthole which was about half their girth. The chief cook, 'Old Vic' as he was generally known, was something of a character. He had already served twenty-five years in the Royal Navy and said he would stay in the service as long as they would have him. He was well read and had a quote for nearly everything that happened.

On Saturdays when the ship was in harbour, the forenoon was taken up with Captain's Rounds when the mess-deck, along with all the other parts of the ship had to be cleaned and polished from deck to deck head (floor to ceiling). To help make things easier all round, the messes would have a cold lunch on Saturday and that was usually corned beef. The first time I delivered the huge tins of 'bully' to the galley, 'Old Vic', with a most scornful look on his face muttered, 'Hebrews, thirteen, eight'. When I asked the supply petty officer what was meant by this quotation he told me to look in the Bible. Sure enough, the book of Hebrews, chapter thirteen, verse eight read 'Jesus Christ, the same yesterday and today and forever'. On another occasion, when we were lined up for a smallpox vaccination 'Old Vic' suggested to the medical officer it was a pity we could not be vaccinated against the 'big' pox!

He liked his pint of beer which always put him in a happy frame of mind, not boisterous but full of mischief which sometimes annoyed the more sober minded amongst his mess mates. If Vic thought that they 'did protest too much' he would exclaim, 'Heaven preserve us from the intolerance of the teetotal'.

Living space in the ship was reckoned at eighteen inches per head but there were always more heads than inches so that some of us had to find sleeping quarters away from the mess. I slung my hammock in the office when we were at sea and on the upper deck when we were in harbour, if the weather was suitable.

The bath room, officially known as the 'wash place' boasted a row of tip-up wash basins which had to be filled from a hot or cold water tap on the bulkhead using the large steel jug provided. At sea, the amount of fresh water was restricted. There was a round shallow steel tub in which you could sit down for a bath if it had not been taken over by somebody washing a blanket, or by an enterprising 'dhobi firm'.

It was quite a spectacle to see two naked men trampling a tub full of washing as if they were pressing grapes, dancing up and down while singing ribald songs to which everyone would join in the chorus. One Geordie Royal Marine used to sing his own version of a pipe tune, 'We are the Irish Jocks. We got no frocks to cover our *****', and a happy-go-lucky young Glasgow-bred stoker, who had an unfortunate speech impediment loved to sing, 'He-he-he-hear m-m-ma s-s-sa-a-n-g — aw shit in the bastard'. We never did hear the rest of his song. Somebody would put on his pseudo Irish voice to warble, 'Oh Danny boy, your oilskin's in the drying room'.

We had not much in the shape of wash powders then so we just used the hard pusser's soap. We often washed our body and teeth with the same coarse detergent. We could buy more civilised toiletries from the N.A.A.F.I. canteen if they were in stock and you had any cash left out of your half-crown a day salary.

It made all the difference in the world if you were able to acquire a bucket which would become a cherished and well guarded possession. There would always be someone wishing to borrow your bucket and if you sensibly rejected his overtures the normal retort would be, 'Shit in it then!' The word 'ess aich one tee' was used quite a lot.

With one pail of hot water you would bathe yourself, wash your clothes and pour the suds over your head and body. You would repeat the process with the rinsing water if you had any. Your clothes were never very dirty because you changed them every day and tried to wash them as you took them off. There were showers available but they were only salt water. Having done your dhobying you had to find somewhere to dry the stuff and it was useful if you had a friend who was a stoker.

Of course, we were all naked in the wash place and there were plenty of personal remarks regarding one's standing in the community such as 'donkey rigged', 'shortie', 'surely had no toys to play with', 'mine's just a wee-en, I use it for pee-en', 'secret weapon' etc. Some chaps who were over well-endowed might be asked if it could pick up peanuts. You could develop quite an inferiority complex! The wash places were not very spacious so you had to choose the best time you could to get your choice of a wash bowl. You would have to walk to and from your mess wearing nothing but a smile or maybe a small towel held in front of you or as some would say, 'Nothing on but the wireless'.

The men's toilets — officially named 'heads' since ancient times — were in the fore part of the ship. They consisted of a row of hand flushed lavatory pans, each separately enclosed from seat to shoulder height and with a door at the front so that you had at least a semblance of privacy. However, you had nowhere to hide and it was easy to count the heads and feet. This 'resting place' was not exactly a fully sound-proofed studio either so you could not help but overhear everybody's conversations as well as various other sobs and sounds which would call for exclamations such as 'Now you're talking', 'Fasten chinstays!' 'Anybody hurt?,' 'Damned good shot, what?' 'Secure for depth charges!'

One stoker seemed to have full control of his downabout ventilating emissions and often produced a series of drum rolls followed by what sounded not unlike 'God save the King'. He was reputed to be able to play 'Bluebells of Scotland' but I never heard that performance.

The standard issue of toilet paper consisted of coarse, thick, brown stuff cut into sheets four inches square and the ration was three sheets per man per day. It was said to be one up, one down and one polishing. Of course there was never enough and you would often hear a poor lost soul pleading with a neighbour for a spare sheet of newspaper or an old letter or something. One despairing voice was heard to ask if anybody had 'two ten shilling notes for a pound'. On one occasion we received a stock of nice, white toilet rolls which did not last very long as the sailors found them ideal for writing air-mail letters.

The able seaman in charge of and responsible for keeping the place clean and tidy had the imposing title of 'Captain of the Heads' and tried to lighten his load by enlisting the help of his 'customers' using notices chalked all over the bulkhead referring to 'high-angled guns — not high angled armholes'. Once he chalked up in a number of places, 'Flush pans after use please' and my goodness, that did appeal to the ingenuity of the sailors. By rubbing out certain letters you could change the wording of the notices to 'Sh. Pa's after us' or 'lush pan aft use please' and many other witticisms. There was the standard notice which hung above the urinal troughs long before the arrival of James Bond and advised, 'Don't kid yourself, stand closer!'

There were several nautical terms for the body functions such as 'pump ship', 'go for a leak', or 'shed a tear for Nelson'. Also men would talk about 'testing dropping gear' while the more politically inclined would refer to the act of 'debating a motion' and others, especially the Irish ratings, might speak of 'going to see the turd engineer'. There was never much need for laxatives aboard an escort ship. There was usually a queue for the heads and one of the most widely used commands was 'Break it off short', an act not easy to perform if we were suffering a bit of 'Gippy tummy' at the time. One chap always wanted to tell the story about the constipated mathematician who worked it out with a pencil.

Eventually our refit was completed and we were ready to get on with the war. We took on a new Captain, Commander, Navigator and Gunnery Officer plus several other officers — all very senior gold braid.

We sailed to Rosyth at the beginning of May and while there we raised the pennon of the Rear Admiral commanding the 20th Cruiser Squadron. We were now the leader of the Gash Boats.

We spent a couple of days in Rosyth which gave us a fine change of scenery. I always liked that part of the world, especially the town of Dunfermline.

By the time we got moving again the fight to save Norway was in full swing and already many ships had been sunk and a lot of lives lost. A visit to Narvik was looked upon almost as a death sentence and we were going to have to take our shot at it, same as everybody else. That was what we joined for — so we were told. At that time there was a popular song called, 'Who's taking you home tonight?' which included the line, 'Who's the lucky boy who's going your way?' Our lads' version was, 'Who's the lucky boy who's going to Norway?'

From Rosyth we steamed to Scapa Flow where we joined up with ships which had returned from Narvik, looking very much 'battered but unbowed'.

Being a flagship meant we had more claimants for the already overcrowded mess decks and officers' quarters. We also had the new R.D.F. operators while some of the living quarters had been converted into offices and workshops. Our regulation eighteen inches of space per man had gone by the board. The primitive wash places and heads were now even less appealing. Some ratings had to share a kit locker.

The wise ones used to say, 'Not to worry. We shall all be in a smaller place yet!'

From Scapa Flow we headed north calling in at Sullom Voe, just to tantalise me I suppose. A few days later we were off the Lofoten Islands escorting shipping in and out of Harstad and Narvik, where the Stukas came thick and fast. We never could get to like those screaming, howling vengeful harpies of Hades.

On the way to Norway we met a convoy of crippled ships under tow, including my old ship *Penelope*, limping their weary way back home after a spell around Narvik. It was not very encouraging for us on our way in. Still — men must work — and all the rest of it.

In Narvik Fjord we spent the day and night enjoying Norway's twenty-four hours' daylight going round and round like a goldfish in a bowl. My old stoker friend Jack put it more colourfully, 'like a turd in a pisspot'. Our engines never stopped and our guns were seldom silent. We were an ideal target for Stukas and J.U. 88 dive-bombers. Even the high-level attackers found us easy to aim for. However, skilled navigation, the use of a bomb sight to predict the direction of falling bombs and the very rapid fire of the four-inch guns putting up a massive barrage of flak kept us, and our charges, mostly unscathed, but we were not allowed much sleep when sunset and dawn seemed to come both at the same time.

On quite a few occasions we tried to load ammunition from a lighter but had to cut the ropes and get away quickly before we even started. The Luftwaffe always seemed to know what we were doing. Then one of our bridge lookouts said that he had noticed a motor cyclist on a nearby hill who would come out of a hut and drive along the hillside whenever we went near an ammunition lighter or an oiler. Next time the cyclist appeared a burst from our pom-pom seemed to discourage him and we managed to fill up our magazines and fuel tanks without much interruption.

It was only when the weather deteriorated and sometimes brought a few hours of low ceiling that we could get on with any normal work. On one such occasion I had to take the motor cutter and a working party to see what could be salvaged from a store ship which had been damaged and forced to run aground. Guess what I brought back? Baa-baa yourself! Another time when everything seemed to be quiet and we had no reports of enemy aircraft, part of our action watch was stood down and most of the lads went straight to the wash place and stripped off for a quick wash. Almost immediately the alarm rattlers screamed and the men had to dash back to their posts. I wondered what would be in the minds of the bomber crews if they came close enough to see that some of the guns were manned by naked men! The gun loaders had to watch what they were taking hold of!

Near the end of May we left Harstad with our sister ship *H.M.S. Cairo* and two Tribal class destroyers and steamed north escorting the heavy cruiser *H.M.S. Effingham* which was loaded with British troops with the intention of landing reinforcements in the port of Bodo. It was a fine clear evening as we steamed on through Bodo Fjord, the powerful *Effingham* leading the squadron. By a wonderful stroke of luck the Luftwaffe were busy elsewhere and left us alone to get on with our work which, for once, the Germans seemed not to know about. I had just come down from my lookout duties at the end of the second dogwatch when we realised something had gone horribly wrong.

With a grinding crash and clouds of dense black smoke the big cruiser drove herself on to a reef which nobody knew was there, and tore the very heart out of her. We turned hard over to avoid ramming her and ran aground ourselves for our trouble. One of the Tribal class destroyers had to copy our mishap and ran aground as well. Jack said it was 'The best "hard on" he'd seen for a long time!'

After much jumping up and down on the quarterdeck like demented chimpanzees we managed to shake ourselves free, coming away with a ruptured fuel tank — not the only thing ruptured that day! The grounded destroyer got herself free but suffered a damaged propeller. We were not too seriously hurt with a bit of luck, but the *Effingham* (sailors had another name for her) was a complete write-off. Fortunately, there were no casualties and we were not spotted by the German forces so we were able to lift off the cruiser's passengers and crew without anybody getting his feet wet, except for one soldier who was full of drink and fell over the side. He was fished out none the worse for wear.

The destroyers ferried the men to other ships and we got under way again on a return journey, standing to action stations all night. We had about twelve hundred British soldiers crammed below decks. We were told by their officers that they had just had supper and would not require being fed so they were left to look after themselves — and didn't they just.

We landed the troops at Harstad the next morning and as there seemed to be no immediate danger of air attack half the watch stood down and went to their mess deck. What a mess they had to face. All the food in the shelves had been devoured. A week's ration of canned fruit and vegetables had been emptied. They must have been hungry!

The British infantryman is probably the bravest and best foot soldier in the world. He has proved his worth all over the globe since times long past despite all that has beset him. The poor old gravel crunchers have had to put up with an awful lot. But these young soldiers, who had been our guests, were inexperienced, poorly equipped and completely demoralised. They had been up against Quisling forces as well as crack German troops so they did not know whom they were fighting and they had no faith at all in their commanders. Whoever was at fault this was not the best of form to say the least, but it certainly opened our eyes to what the other Services were coping with.

As soon as we had disembarked our passengers and tidied the mess decks up a bit we moved to Lavangs Fjord to refuel from a tanker which was under attack most of the time from both high-level and dive-bombers. For the next week, night and day in the land of the midnight sun we, and the rest of the 20th Cruiser Squadron, endured repeated bombing. We were getting rid of thousands of rounds of four-inch and pom-pom ammunition every two or three days so that we were clearing our deck lockers and magazines almost faster than we could replenish them. We also had to take the chance of keeping the ammunition barge alongside and hope that we could prevent her being blown up and us along with her. Then every available man had to go like the clappers to heave the shells aboard and get them stored. It was some job but, tired as we were, we managed somehow.

Stocking up the magazines was not an easy task, but getting the shells to the quick-firing guns was a performance that the best of stage farces could not have equalled. There was a chute from the magazine in the bowels of the ship going up to the deck space or 'flat' which was closest to the gun mountings. My action station when I was not up aloft was the sickbay flat which appeared to be so called because the sickbay was there. From the deck head above the chute was suspended a wooden pulley block through which was passed a rope. One end of the rope was attached to a metal frame called a 'cruet' which held four fixed ammunition four-inch calibre shells while the other end went round the driving wheel of the electric motor in the magazine below. The shells were sent up on the cruet to the flat and the supply party would take them from there to the gun deck by hand. If one shell had slipped from its not very safe hold it could have blown up the magazine and the rest of us with it. The Admiral would not have liked that! When the gun crews required ammunition, shouted commands had to be relayed to the men down below, usually cooks, stewards or supply ratings.

Those who thought up these anti-aircraft ships believed that small ammunition lockers beside the guns would hold plenty of shells to support whatever barrage was required to destroy the two or three high-level bombers attacking the convoy, and the supply parties would then be able to replace the stocks as soon as the action ceased.

As usual, the experts knew Sweet Fanny Adams about it!

In the real world the dive-bombers and torpedo-bombers came in thick and fast and our guns developed a ferocious appetite which we had to satisfy with all the speed we could muster. I thought the quickest way to deliver the goods after I had shouted down the chute, 'Send them up, Freddie', or something similar, was to run up the ladder to the gun deck and bend double over the guardrail to grab each shell as it was lifted up to me. I then passed it on to one of the gun crew who shoved it into the rack. Very often there was not even time for that and I just handed the overgrown bullet direct to the loader who had it fused, loaded and fired by the time I came with the next one. It was very good exercise for the stomach muscles if you cared for that sort of thing but I had never planned to be a weight-lifter and after an hour or two of this routine the shells seemed to be as heavy as me.

These same planners also believed that we would always face the enemy head on or broadside and the ships were armed accordingly. But these German airmen did not play the game by our rules and preferred to attack a ship from astern, straight out of the sun if possible, bless you Jack and all the rest of it. This meant that the after guns were the first to run out of ammunition and had to be provided from the forward magazines by the good old forward supply party. The only way we could manage this operation was for each of us to put a shell on his shoulder and run as fast as a tomcat with two yards start on the vet, at the same time trying to keep our balance on the tossing, jumping deck taking cover whenever possible, while the shrapnel from falling flak or near misses seemed to be seeking each of us out for its own amusement.

What a bleedin' performance!

Since it came to be my duty to lead the way I was eternally grateful to the stoker who always ran along with me. Jack, who came from Wigan, was a natural comic — everything he said was funny. It was a great morale-booster to hear him reciting the Naval version of the epic poems written by Robert Service or Rudyard Kipling, hardly pausing for breath, except to utter a four letter word when something nasty came whizzing over our heads a wee bit close as we struggled our way to the quarterdeck and back. He was also right with me whenever we had to carry out our emergency duties such as tying up or letting go moorings while the seamen, who normally did the work, were too busy firing the guns for their more mundane jobs.

Jack was a laugh a minute. He had a daytime job as chief stoker's messman and when he came to collect their rum ration he could not just call out the mess number like everybody else, but had to come out with a long spiel, 'Jack Tar, R.F.R., thirty-eight, Tiffies' mate, always late, make him wait'. When he had collected the issue he would leave with the parting words, 'I shall go now, but if I should return in my absence, please detain me until I get back when I shall deal with me, wilt tha?' If somebody tried to make fun of him he would say, 'You can go and piss up my back and see how I like it, wilt tha?' Jack usually ended a sentence with 'Wilt tha?'

I learned a great deal from dear old Jack and I fairly missed him after he left the ship.

During brief spells when the bombers were less persistent, British Army Royal Engineers assisted by Royal Marines from *H.M.S. Curlew* managed to construct a landing strip at nearby Skaanland and a few Gloucester Gladiators and Hurricanes were able to come to our help. They were hopelessly outnumbered but it did make a difference. One fighter was worth a lot of guns — but don't tell that to the Admirals! Unfortunately they arrived too late to prevent *Curlew* being blown to bits before the disbelieving eyes of the men who had just completed work on the temporary runway. *Cairo* was also damaged but managed to carry on.

By this stage we were urgently needing to clean boilers and to re-line some of the guns. The only way we could get peace to do this was to steam away somewhere up around the North Cape into a blizzard so that we could shut down one boiler at a time, letting the stokers slave away at the scraping and chipping as soon as it was cool enough. Not the regulation way of doing things but some of us also managed to get a few hours' rest at the same time. Forty-eight hours later we were back in the thick of it.

It was planned that a force of British, French and Norwegian troops would invade, capture and destroy Narvik to deny its use to the enemy and for this a good bombardment was essential. The question was who did we have to do the shooting? There was only one heavy cruiser left in the area so the two ant-aircraft ships had to use our high-angled guns to fire at the shore installations. This was not a very easy task. The men had to reach above their heads to load the guns. Salvos from shore batteries splashed in the water just short of us but we were not hit. I don't suppose we hit anything either.

Fighter planes from the newly built airstrip had temporarily won control of the cloudless sky so that we were able to carry out the bombardment and land the troops in peace. But in the early morning, fog grounded our own fighter aircraft and the waiting J.U. 88s came tearing in like dogs at dinnertime.

Our luck still held but the other ships were not so fortunate. *H.M.S. Cairo* received two direct hits causing a number of casualties. She survived the onslaught but had to be sent home, stopping on the way to bury her dead. She took the survivors from *Curlew* home with her.

So far, we had lost only one man through enemy action. Our sister ships had spent more time here than we had and had been fighting in this beautiful deadly place while we were still undergoing repairs, but a few of the lads were already becoming a bit 'bomb happy'. We could do with a night's sleep and we were longing for a decent meal. In the thick of the day-to-day action, three of us had to sit a written examination for supply petty officer which had to be taken on the specified date or not at all, regardless of circumstances! The show must go on! Therefore Pete, 'Spud', and I sat ourselves down in separate offices and spent the day trying to concentrate on the unfamiliar questions whilst listening to the blasts of gunfire above us and the thumps and shudders of near misses exploding in the water. Pete, who took everything in his stride, passed with flying colours but 'Spud' and I would have to wait until next year — or maybe the year after that. We should not have been fighting when there were exams to sit!

There must have been previous experience of continuous day and night action but none of us knew of any instructions laid down with regard to feeding the men at their action stations, particularly on an old ship like this on 'canteen messing' where each mess was geared to look after its own catering. Until the Invergordon Mutiny in the late twenties their Lordships had not considered the welfare of the lower deck sailors to be of any particular importance. They had allowed the men a ration of essential victuals which was considered enough to keep them fighting fit and expected them to be jolly well grateful for it. After Invergordon, new ships were fitted out with a proper galley staffed by trained cooks, and sailors were given a varied menu with a proper balanced diet. They were not exactly overfed but at least they had sufficient — and sometimes more than most of them had been used to in Civvy Street.

The chief cook and the supply chief had to figure out some sort of meal which could be devoured by the men during a brief lull in the battle. Soup would have been a good 'filler' but we had no means of cooking and serving it up so it was decided that the best idea would be sandwiches, lots and lots of sandwiches, with either tea, coffee or cocoa. Our tough old bakers could produce any amount of the finest bread whatever the conditions. There was plenty of corned beef in the hold and, even better still, we had a load of tinned skinless sausages which we had salvaged from a damaged stores ship recently. Whenever we had a quiet spell we set about slicing, spreading and brewing like a frenzy of Women's Institute ladies at a jubilee jamboree. The doorstep sandwiches may not have been suitable for a Royal garden party, but the eagerly awaited sustenance was appreciated by those to whom it was delivered by the sturdy vassals of the forward supply party moving as quickly as their tired legs would allow.

For strategic reasons the rum issue had to be delayed until the second dogwatch when it was usually possible to stand down a few of the hands at a time.

When I suggested to the chief pusser that there was no standard accountancy procedure for this method of victualling, and our actions would probably make the pen-pushers at Whitehall demand that we be hung from the highest yardarm in the British navy, his unconcerned reply was, 'We have an Admiral on board and that old bugger can easily sign something'.

In the midst of all this stramash the unsung hero of the day was the N.A.A.F.I. canteen manager. He was an elderly retired man who had volunteered his services as soon as war broke out. A kindly, moderate person, he was probably the oldest man on the ship, and a civilian at that, yet he dashed around from the bridge to the bilges, wherever men were on duty. He carried a suitcase packed with cigarettes, chocolate and any other item he thought the sailors might require. If they did not have the ready cash he would accept their word that they would see him later. I don't think anyone let him down. His little suitcase seemed to carry everything and, for a wager, somebody asked him for a back collar stud which he produced without a twinkle of an eye.

The men looked forward to seeing his cheery face and he was probably the best pick-me-up the ship's company ever had. He lived in the chief petty officer's mess and when he left the ship on our return to the U.K., his mess mates gave him a lovely handmade scroll of appreciation which he said he would treasure for the rest of his life. Such men are never considered to be heroes. I wonder why?

By the end of May we had gone three weeks with hardly a wink of sleep. We became so tired that if we had a quiet moment we just dozed off wherever we were. We hardly dared to take off our clothes which were only underpants a boiler suit and gym shoes but we tried to get a bit of a wash whenever we could. It was remarkable how we seemed to become wide-awake as soon as the guns opened fire.

The worst of it was that we had no idea what was going on outside our own little world. Those in charge must have believed that we were too dumb to be told anything. Of course, many officers in all the services at the start of the war were as thick as two planks themselves. They had a standard reply if asked anything, 'You are not paid to think. Do as you are told and get on with your work'.

Unknown to us here in Norway, Hitler's troops had started to attack the west and had very quickly overrun Belgium, Holland and half of France. A British rescue fleet made up of warships, merchant ships and hundreds of small civilian pleasure craft had lifted off a large part of the British Expeditionary Force from the beaches of Dunkirk and other places. Among the rescuers was our sister ship *Calcutta* whom we had thought was still around here with us.

The top brass here knew what they were doing — we supposed. H.Q. had already decided to end the battle the men had believed they were winning and planned to withdraw the British and French forces from Norway, leaving the Norwegian army to hold on as long as possible, until they were forced to capitulate. They did not tell the Norwegians either, having been taught to be cautious.

At the end of May we started the evacuation. It was our first experience of this development in modern warfare. It was not going to be our last.

We began taking loaded ships out and empty ships in. We had to confuse the enemy whose grand fleet was hanging around waiting for us. We also had to hide our intentions from the poor unsuspecting soldiers of the gallant Norwegian Army who were trying to hold back the advancing Germans.

Probably the most confused people were ourselves.

For the first week of June we provided cover for the small ships carrying the Allied troops from the shore to the troopers. We acted as a staging post while this was going on. Amongst those we had aboard temporarily was a French Foreign Legion Alpine Unit. I managed to converse a little with one of those tough fighters. He said they were surprised that they had had to spike some of the British guns which had just been abandoned and left to the enemy. Another of these chaps had taken the identity discs from all the Germans he had killed and had them attached to his waist as if he were a Red Indian with enemy scalps. Actually he was of Polish nationality.

Eventually, in early June, after we had gathered in all the allied soldiers we could find we left And Fjord with two destroyers to join forces with a convoy of eight transports carrying about ten thousand men. With them were a heavy cruiser, an aircraft carrier, and seven destroyers. A County class cruiser carrying the Norwegian Royal Family raced on ahead. In the convoy was a transport ship filled with German prisoners of war, and for reasons known only to Hermann Wilhelm Goering and his Luftwaffe pilots this particular vessel seemed to be the main target for the high-level bombers, so we had to defend the bloody enemy as well!

The German fleet including *Scharnhorst* and *Gneisenau* failed to find us for which we uttered many a prayer of thanks. They did make contact with the aircraft carrier *Glorious* and her escorts and blew them all out of the water — killing about two thousand men. These included the brave Royal Air Force pilots who had flown their Hurricanes and Gladiators from the new airstrip at Skaanland and succeeded in landing them on the carrier's flight deck. It was a skilful and daring operation but it was all for nothing.

As usual, the British Home Fleet was searching in the wrong part of the war area at the time.

After a few days of long-range bombing attacks and the occasional U-boat scare we shepherded the convoy into the Clyde where we anchored in the safe port of Greenock. There we spent the next two days cleaning the ship and taking on stores and ammunition.

We had surely served our apprenticeship now!

The rest of Britain had learned a thing or two as well. The war had only just started and already we had our backs to the wall. Neville Chamberlain's government caved in and had to be re-organised into a coalition under the leadership of Winston Churchill with Clem Atlee as his deputy. He promised us blood, toil, tears and sweat and he was not far wrong. We certainly had plenty of sweat, anyway.

A few officers and ratings were sent to hospital suffering from stress and exhaustion — some said 'bomb happy'! Everybody's nerves were a bit frayed by now but a night ashore in Glasgow with a visit to the famous long bar helped to revive our drooping spirits. It is wonderful what a drop of the amber liquid can do for a body.

Rear Admiral Vivian transferred his flag to *H.M.S. Cairo* after saying goodbye and telling us he would not recommend anybody in the squadron for a decoration but he would ask that we should all be given a good spell of leave. So we sailed around to Wallsend on Tyne shipyard and were granted three days' leave each watch, half of which was spent travelling and the rest of it sleeping.

Wallsend was the yard where this ship was born so it was fitting that she should be sent back there for treatment in her declining years. We sojourned there for about three weeks which included a spell in dry dock where we could not use our own 'heads'. We were allowed to go to the toilets provided for the shipyard workers and I was intrigued on entering the hallowed edifice by way of a turnstile controlled by an unhappy looking clerk behind a small window who appeared to be clocking us in and out. 'Wee Jimmy' who was a 'dockyard matey' by profession told us that 'the regulation time allowed for a sh*te was ten minutes and if it took you any longer you forfeited half-an-hour's wages which in his case as an apprentice was about one penny but it could be as much as ninepence for a journeyman'.

We had a few runs ashore into Newcastle which was a great town with several theatres, some grand new cinemas and lots of fine pubs. The Geordies were wonderful people who went out of their way to make the sailors welcome and we had plenty of fun. One evening, when travelling on a crowded bus, a young supply rating mess mate of ours whom we called 'Witty' was somewhat taken aback when the woman sitting next to him began to breast feed her baby. The bairn did not seem to fancy his menu and she said in a loud whisper, 'If ye dinna take it I'll give it to this gentleman here.'

His face was even more crimson when he alighted from the bus to a rousing cheer from his fellow travellers.

By the end of June we were back in Scapa Flow. I had now been relieved of my extra duties as anti-aircraft lookout and was a bit sad about it because later I missed a lot of fun.

We were taken over by another First Lieutenant. This fellow was an old sea dog of the 'give 'em the cold steel' school. He had been put on the shelf after the Great War and recalled to service in 1939. He was a bluff, hearty hard-drinking officer of the type who was made the hero of many a romantic seagoing adventure story since the time of Nelson. The lower deck did not think very highly of officers generally but this 'old duffer' turned out to be the sort of leader you could follow — if he did not go too fast. The most cynical of old-timers had respect and even affection for him. Being 'ancient' himself he had a soft spot for the older generation of ratings but not a lot of time for the younger ones unless they were good athletes. He regarded only seamen and stokers as being the 'real navy'. The rest of us were just newfangled necessities that had to be endured.

Our next task was to escort four converted ferries which were laying mines all around Orkney and Shetland. The weather was ideal for airborne attack but we did not meet with much opposition. Perhaps the enemy were as scared as we were when half the mines exploded as soon as they hit the water. Then it was back again to Scapa Flow along with units of the Home Fleet. There were also several decoy ships there, including the ancient battleship *H.M.S. Iron Duke*, but this did not fool the enemy as there were no seabirds flying around them. When this fact dawned upon the 'brainy ones', sailors were put aboard with the sole duty of throwing out 'gash' to attract the gulls.

We were in a sort of limbo at this stage. The Germans now had control of the coastline from the Bay of Biscay to the North Cape and we expected them to invade Britain at any time. We had no idea as to where the main forces would land and the Northern Isles were considered to be well on the cards.

As it turned out later, because of the bluff and guts of the defending forces, especially our fighter pilots, the Germans were unable to get command of the sky and had to forget about the invasion, but after the Royal Navy's experience at Narvik and Dunkirk we could be forgiven for thinking we had no Royal Air Force left!

After two days in Scapa Flow we picked up the minelayers again and guarded them as they laid their 'eggs' in the Irish Sea between Anglesey and Dublin. We then steamed around the corner and straight on to Plymouth where we moored next to our sister ship *H.M.S. Calcutta*, now repaired and restored after her experiences off the coast of France. Both of us were in action that night helping to defend the dockyard which had become the target for regular nightly air raids.

H.M.S. Coventry and *Calcutta* were soon to become the 'terrible twins'.

It was our first experience of seeing bombs fall among our own civilian population and it gave us an ominous feeling of what was to come.

Next day we were granted seven days' leave each watch.

Being second watch for leave I had a chance of a run ashore at night. It was glorious weather and I had intended to do some sightseeing. I had always been fond of walking but the sight of the bomb-damaged town rather dampened my enthusiasm so I ended up in a Plymouth public house where I had my initiation in the local pastime of drinking scrumpy — the real stuff!

The effect was mortal! Going back to the dockyard I had difficulty pushing away the pavement which kept rolling up towards my feet and I could not make up my mind whether to duck under the telephone wires or step over them. Next morning I learned the real punishment for my sins when

I went to the heads and became convinced I had swallowed a lot of broken glass. No wonder Francis Drake wanted to chase Spanish Armadas all over the place.

Must have been his bowls!

While we were in Devonport dockyard some of the men who had been with us since the beginning of the war were drafted to other parts. They were now veterans and were required to train new entries. Some were put ashore because of their age, including the respected and well-liked Engineer Commander for whom I used to wangle a pound or two of leaf tobacco which one of the stokers rolled for him. I enjoyed listening to his yarns about 1914 and the years before. Once I offended him by writing in the space for his signature for oil fuel the title, 'Commander (E)' instead of 'Engineer Commander'! In a voice filled with sadness and nostalgia he said, 'For C*****'s sake, give me my proper rank. There's not many of us old buggers left now'. He belonged to the old school of engineers who served their time in the shipyards before going to sea. This tough old chap had kept the ship's engines going through some hard times.

Another bunch of recruits joined us to learn about a life on the ocean wave, and we were now a proper 'multi-racial society' with men from England, Scotland, Wales, Northern and Southern Ireland, the Isle of Wight, Cornwall and Yorkshire; there was even an American on the seamen's messdeck. He was a fellow who had been in England on business in 1939 and had volunteered his services to the Royal Navy long before America came into the war. I do not remember his name but for some reason we called him 'Yank'. He became one of the lads although he was older than many of us.

We were soon under way again making for the Clyde along with *Calcutta* and spent a couple of nights in Greenock where we picked up some passengers for our next destination. We were left to guess where that might be but no doubt there would be plenty of bombers to entertain us.

It was about the third week in August when we steamed west to join a convoy of four large merchant ships in the company of a battle wagon, two carriers, three cruisers, and six destroyers and we were told we were going to join the Mediterranean Fleet. On the way we picked up and buried the two-man crew of a Fulmar fighter plane from one of the aircraft carriers who had crash landed in the sea and lost their lives. It did not make a good start to our newest expedition.

After a fairly trouble-free journey we arrived at Gibraltar just twelve months since we first visited the place as a bunch of 'rookies' on a training exercise in peacetime. Was that really only one year ago? Already it was beginning to seem like a long war.

The next morning we headed for Malta to land our passengers. Malta was already showing the scars of repeated bombing. Italy was now our enemy but did very little to interfere with our journey. Inquisitive aircraft were driven off by our fighters from the two big aircraft carriers and the Italian fleet kept well away to the north showing no inclination to mix it with us. The Nazi French fleet at Oran had earlier been rendered harmless by the action of Admiral Somerville with Force H.

There had been an air raid on Valletta not long before we arrived and we were cheered into the Grand Harbour by a large number of local people lining the ramparts singing their war chant: 'Raiders past, kiss my arse. F*** Mussolini!' The name Mussolini seemed to have a grand operatic sound when fittingly connected to the four-letter expletive!

After a few hours in Malta we left to become part of the Eastern Mediterranean Fleet under the command of Admiral Cunningham. A bit later on we came under attack by a large force of Italian heavy bombers and fighters. They were quickly dispersed by our own fighters from the aircraft carrier *Illustrious* and we suffered only a few not very near misses.

With four destroyers, we and our other half, *H.M.S. Calcutta*, left the main fleet to escort six merchant ships bound for various ports in the Gulf of Athens. At dawn we were attacked by twelve Italian high-level bombers but they were only amateurs and were easily deterred by our experienced gunners.

We left the convoy as it approached its home port and we joined up with ships of the Cruiser Squadron looking for Mussolini's warships which had already performed the great Italian vanishing act. That suited us as we did not like them anyway so we rejoined *Calcutta* and the two of us escorted a convoy of empty ships returning from Greek ports to Egypt. After a few uninteresting high-level attacks we reached Alexandria safely and tied up to the Kamari mole which was to be our regular berth from then on. *H.M.S. Calcutta* tied up astern of us.

The harbour was very busy and filled with shipping including two Vichy French battleships now demilitarised and under guard. They had been our allies at the start of the war. We were given a few hours' shore leave into Alexandria but the city did not seem to be as friendly as it had been a year ago. It was now involved in a war which had really nothing to do with the Egyptians — apart from the money they made out of it.

The next morning we said cheerio to *Calcutta* and made speed for Port Said and then through the Suez Canal to escort a slow convoy to Aden.

It was very hot in the Red Sea and the Gulf of Suez and sea water had to be pumped over the deck in the daytime to make it a bit more kind to our feet. Awnings were rigged wherever convenient and a canvas bath filled with sea water was fitted in the port waist so that men could take a dip to cool their overheated bodies. Not long ago we had been trying to keep ourselves warm in the northern hemisphere. Never mind, our winter woollies would be arriving any minute now!

The whole trip to Aden was uneventful although we were at action stations all night while we steamed past the Italian occupied port of Massawa. We also provided cover for ships leaving British Somaliland which country was about to be taken over by the Black Shirts. Our High Command considered it was not worth hanging on to at the moment. It was our third 'evacuation' of the War but not very exciting.

We stayed a few hours looking at the barren rocks of Aden and then escorted a convoy to Port Sudan where we were allowed a few hours ashore. Port Sudan was a small trading post with not too much in the shape of hotels or bars. The management was mostly Egyptian and the workforce fuzzy-wuzzies with bones through their noses and all the rest of it. It did not take some of our London-born ratings long to teach these fierce warriors how to do the Lambeth Walk — spears and all, helped of course by the effect of the local brew. Next day we left with another convoy to Aden. On the way we came across some Arabian dhows which had to be brought alongside and searched for contraband, spies or slaves. Since nobody amongst our ship's company admitted to speaking Arabic and the crews aboard the dhows claimed to have no English we could not say that the operation was a great success and we had to watch them sail gracefully on their way. A few hours later we were attacked by three Italian pre-war biplanes who dropped what appeared to be do-it-yourself bombs nowhere near us. Shortly afterwards we were in Aden harbour and were granted a few hours' shore leave.

Aden was a small Crown Colony taken by Britain from the Turks a hundred years previously and used originally as a coaling stop, but was now an oil fuel depot. There was not much entertainment on offer except a few small bazaars, a fenced-off swimming area, and a N.A.A.F.I. bar where you could buy a glass of Egyptian onion beer, if you could manage to acquire a drinking glass which was nothing more than a beer bottle cut off at the shoulders. The beer tasted like something to do with camels but the flies enjoyed it!

For the next three days we were at sea steaming up and down the Eritrean coast and then we returned to Aden where we joined forces with *H.M.S. Ajax* to escort three large troopships filled with Australian and New Zealand infantrymen bound for Suez and the British Desert Army.

By the end of September we were back in our usual billet in Alexandria, having sweated off every ounce of surplus flesh we had and maybe more.

Two days later we set off to join up with the First Battle Squadron covering convoys to Greece and looking for Italian convoys to Libya. After two or three days of this we returned to Alexandria where we were given all night leave to one watch. It was grand to sleep in a proper bed and have the use of a real bathroom again. The city was blessed with a large number of tourist hotels. These used to be kept for the 'posh' folks but with the lack of holiday trade they were available to any of the sailors who were prepared to pay for them and it was worth a week's pay for a few hours' kip on a nice clean bed!

The second week of October saw us tied up once more preparing to paint the ship's side which was sorely needed. We were still sporting the Atlantic dark grey colour. A competition had been set to see who amongst the ship's company could design the best camouflage pattern, and an able seaman of the London R.N.V.R. who was an artist by profession had produced what was considered to be the most suitable.

But the 'Buffer' had to postpone his exterior redecoration yet again when the whole fleet left harbour to escort a convoy of supplies and reinforcements to Malta which was now being besieged by the Italian navy and air force. We joined with *Calcutta* to provide anti-aircraft cover. Apart from U-boat scares and the ever-present shadowing aircraft we reached Malta without much bother and left with a small convoy of empty ships. A few hours later we were attacked by a large force of Italian bombers who came rather close with their near misses. We spent most of the next day at action stations as we picked up another convoy coming out of Greece.

After we left them, the fleet was in action further north and the old stringback Swordfish planes dropped heavy loads of bombs all over the Italian held Dodecanese Islands' airstrips. Italian torpedo-bombers scored a direct hit on the heavy cruiser *H.M.S. Liverpool* causing severe damage and many casualties. We two anti-aircraft cruisers were detached from the convoy and sent to defend the damaged *Liverpool* which was being towed by the cruiser *H.M.S. Orion*. We got there in time to help drive off a determined attack by more of the same breed.

The Italians had now started bombing the harbour at nights which kept us on our toes during the middle watch. Along with *Calcutta* we were moored near to the harbour entrance so on most nights it fell to us to be the first to open fire. They did not appear to do much damage with their bombs but we had to watch out for the mines which they dropped all around the boom defences. We got used to it.

We had the feeling we should be safe enough as long as it was the Italians who did the bombing. Although some of their airmen were brave and skilful — particularly their torpedo men — we did not have a great deal of respect for them away from their ice-cream barrows!

We stayed in Alexandria for the next week. We had lots of work to do but it was a fairly restful time. Despite the air raids we managed to enjoy a few nights' shore leave.

This time, the First Lieutenant was able to get all the available hands on to painting the ship's side. They slapped on the newly designed camouflage pattern which was so effective that liberty men coming back to the ship after leave was ended gave the excuse that the ship had been so well disguised that they could not find her — and the officer of the watch believed them! When the officer said, 'Absentee' one man said, 'No thanks, I'm going for'ard to have some cocoa'.

Our 'Tiffies' and 'Chippies' were able to complete a few much needed repairs and maintenance jobs. The ship's boxing team won all their contests and Paddy and company were already proving themselves the best in the Middle East. Our football team also did very well for themselves. Being no athlete myself I was just a good spectator.

Near the end of October 1940, events in the Eastern Mediterranean took a dramatic turn. The great dictator Benito 'Muscle-only' decided to declare war on poor little undefended Greece in the fond belief that his own invincible, highly trained, numerically superior army would be able to walk over the border from Albania and Athens would be at his feet. The tough little Greek Army had other ideas and gave the barbarian Black Shirts a very sharp kick in the places they did not care to speak about.

The Greeks were quite prepared to sort out this bunch of hokey-pokey merchants but they needed help from us in the form of arms and equipment so we were soon busy escorting very slow convoys of ships carrying vital supplies. To control this action we had to set up a naval base in the port of Athens and a transit depot in the harbour of Suda Bay on the island of Crete.

The fleet was busy on the west side of Crete looking for Mussolini's warships. His Admirals always knew when it was a good time to stay at home!

We were just getting settled in Suda Bay when we were attacked by a large formation of heavy bombers, but despite the Italians' repeated assaults, the combined barrage from the three cruisers was enough to send them back to whence they came with one of their aircraft missing. Next day we steamed back to Alexandria and came out with two convoys — one with vital supplies for Malta and the other with an oil tanker and a detachment of Royal Artillery with their guns and equipment for Suda Bay. We left the gunners in the care of *H.M.S. Calcutta* while we carried on with our charges to Malta.

The fleet with *H.M.S. Illustrious* and her fighter aircraft, such as they were, were not far away and we had a fairly uneventful journey to Malta where we spent one night and then made our way back to Egypt (the lads called it 'Egg-wiped') with four merchant ships and a few new ships for Admiral Cunningham's fleet, which was busy at the time knocking seven bells out of some of Benito's battleships at Taranto.

A few days later we were off on what we thought would be another Malta convoy and we had the whole fleet with us. Then we found out that we were going west of Malta escorting the old, worn-out battle-wagon *H.M.S. Ramilles* and two damaged heavy cruisers on their way home for a refit. We were going to meet with Force H who would take over our charges and pass on to us two heavy cruisers who were carrying a large number of soldiers and supplies for the Desert Army. It was kept secret from us but, of course, the Italian navy knew all about it.

While we pressed on to meet with Force H the Italian fleet came out to intercept us and as usual their warships failed to come within range of our big guns. But the Italian air force found us and bombed us fairly accurately bringing about a number of near misses. We had a few fast heartbeats when we saw the aircraft carrier *H.M.S. Ark Royal* — pride of the fleet at that time — vanish behind a wall of water caused by bomb splashes, and there were many sighs of relief when she came through unmarked. In due course Admiral Somerville turned west with his new charges and we turned east with ours, taking the merchant ships to Malta. Then we rejoined the Eastern Mediterranean Fleet and headed for Alexandria which was now almost regarded as our home port. It had not been a bad trip after all.

When we got back we learned that General Wavell had started his rout of the pride of Mussolini's desert army. The Italian soldiers were stalwart and bold against the Ethiopian spear but not very keen on the British or Anzac bayonet and they certainly did not care for the Gurkha kukri. They surrendered in droves!

We were given the task of providing anti-aircraft protection for Royal Navy monitors. These were flat-bottom river boats — just self-propelled gun platforms — which performed valiant service bombarding Italian army positions from close inshore, in and around Sollum and Sidi Barrani.

On the evening of Friday the thirteenth of December 1940 — a date engraved on quite a few memories — we were patrolling alone, without any anti-submarine protection, off the coast of Mersa Matruh. Visibility was not very good due to offshore sandstorms so that our lookouts could not see much further than their noses. Then, just after the first watch had taken over at twenty hundred hours, the sky suddenly cleared and for a little while we were silhouetted against a bright moon, sticking out like a sore thumb to a doctor, camouflaged or not. Sitting in my office, I saw the lights dip and heard the soft whine of the pom-pom motors on 'B' gun deck, two decks above. I was finishing off the day's accounts, it was a fine calm night, and I remember the song we were hearing on the mess deck wireless at the time. It was 'If I Only Had Wings'.

Suddenly there was one hell of a bang and the ship came to a jarring halt. If you have ever been driving a motor car in a head-on collision you will know the feeling. Especially if you have false teeth!

The Commander of an Italian submarine had seen us lying there bare and blue and felt that he just had to send a torpedo in our direction. It scored a hit on our port bow, blowing a dirty great hole above and below the waterline.

As we picked ourselves up from wherever we had landed, nobody had any idea of what had happened but quickly and quietly, without any orders, we went to our action stations. We still remembered Narvik. The Damage Control Party had not before met with this kind of destruction but they had been well trained and knew what to do. With a collision mat around the outside and the hole stuffed with lashed up hammocks and anything else they could get their hands on and shored up with timber they managed to keep out most of the water. The rest could be handled as long as the pumps kept going.

The Captain then brought the ship around and we steamed stern first to Alexandria. Fortunately it was a fine calm night and we were able to secure to our normal berth the next morning.

The punch-line was that the Italian submarine commander was so elated he could not resist the urge to surface and break radio silence. While reporting to his Admiral that he had just sunk a large British cruiser his signals were picked up by our wireless operators and two destroyers, racing to our assistance, caught the U-boat on the surface and sank it, taking the Captain and most of the crew prisoners. The Italians were taken into Alexandria where we were pointed out to them looking as if we did not have a care in the world. The poor old submariner did not know what he had done wrong!

Next day we went into Gabari dry dock to assess the damage. When the water had been drained from the dock and the ship settled down on the stocks it could be seen that we had taken a right biff on the nose. From the waterline down, eighteen feet of the bow had been taken away like a huge bite leaving a gaping hole in the stem which looked as if a mad dentist had been around with a pair of gigantic pliers.

It had not done much for the new paintwork either!

Admiral Cunningham came along, all dressed up in his shining whites, to have a look at the pretty hole but left without as much as a 'How's yer father?' One of the retinue — a sailor who had been standing next to the great man at the time — spread the buzz that it was the Admiral's opinion that the ship could not be spared so she must be patched-up and kept going for as long as she could stay afloat, and the best of luck to us!

A few hours later we were all alone in the port when the fleet left with another convoy for Malta. This time *Calcutta* would have to do our share of the work as well as her own. By now, German aircraft were beginning to show themselves around Greece and Crete.

We stayed in the primitive dry dock for several days while a very much makeshift patch was riveted over the hole. That was long enough to give us Christmas Day ashore and it happened at the same time that there was a lull in enemy aircraft activity. I don't know why the Italian air force did not finish us off then while we were so vulnerable, but instead they gave us a break for a bit of Christmas pudding which, we thought, was jolly decent of them!

It was the normal practice for ratings of each mess to try to save something out of their standard ration issue and victualling allowance during the latter part of the year, so that they could splash out a little on Christmas Day. That was each mess except the notorious number fourteen. They ate and spent as they got and to hell with tomorrow, so they had nothing for their

Christmas dinner. Not to worry. The chief petty officers had purchased a lovely big leg of pork which had been pre-cooked on Christmas Eve and stowed in the galley pantry for reheating the next day. Late at night some of the lads managed to unlock the cupboard door and 'rescue' this succulent offering which they sliced up and made into sandwiches with bread which had also been 'liberated'. The sandwiches were hidden away and never found — despite a diligent search by the Master-at-Arms and his merry men. The poor old chief petty officers had to make do with corned beef but the seamen's mess were all right Jack!

When the same lads went ashore on Christmas afternoon they had no money to spend but none of them came back sober!

Two days later when it was deemed that the repairs had been completed we put to sea for a trial run. We faced a force eight gale for about an hour then the new plates fell off and the Captain had to turn the ship round and keep her afloat until we got back to port. The next day we were again in dry dock where we stayed for three weeks while a more effective repair was made. Angle-iron was welded into what was left of the stem while thin bow plates were welded and riveted to form an outer skin, the deck above was shored up with wooden props, and the hole filled with concrete.

We were seaworthy though not exactly 'Bristol fashion'. Our speed was reduced to about twenty knots. We could not face any sort of gale, nor use our anchors and we had no paravanes to protect us from mines. The sheered off bows made her dip more at sea and the forecastle was always wet. The old hands had a saying, 'Never mind. Worse things happen at sea'.

Living in a ship in dry dock is not the most luxurious accommodation at the best of times but Gabari dock was nothing much more than a hole in the ground in the desert. We could not use our own lavatories and had to put up with two raised planks of wood with buckets underneath inside a tent. Units of the Egyptian Army provided sentries around the docks but we had to put our own guards around the latrines because many of those worthy sons of the desert were always on the lookout for some unwary infidel with his trousers down!

During our spell in dock the whole situation in the Eastern Mediterranean had changed drastically. In the desert, General Wavell's army was still chasing away the Italians as fast as they could run and was having to cope with many thousands of prisoners. Further to the north the gallant little Greek army had succeeded in repulsing the invading Italian hordes and pushed them back into Albania almost to the sea. The convoys and their escort ships had not been unduly harassed by the Italian Air Force and the Italian fleet always came off worst whenever it attempted to mix it with our big ships.

Then Adolph Hitler decided that it was time for him to take charge of that liability Benito's ailing forces. He moved his Flieger Korps X crack bomber squadrons to Italian bases in Sicily and the island of Rhodes.

Early in January 1941 the convoy to Malta covered by the whole fleet was attacked by a large force of Stukas and J.U.88s recognised immediately by our chums on *H.M.S. Calcutta* as those who had caused so much havoc in and around Narvik and Dunkirk. In two days of action one heavy cruiser was badly damaged and another one crippled so that she had to be sunk. One battleship was damaged but was able to carry on fighting and our only large aircraft carrier received six direct hits and just managed to make it into Malta. Despite day and night air raids the dock workers were able to patch her up and get her safely away to Gibraltar. My brother-in-law Alfred was serving as able seaman aboard the carrier at the time. Thankfully he lived to tell the tale.

In forty-eight hours the Eastern Mediterranean Fleet had been severely mauled and suffered many casualties in ships and men. We had also lost the vital support of our only serviceable aircraft carrier with her fighter planes.

We ought to have been sharing in that battle but we were still in dry dock when the grim news came to us. When we were refloated and went back to the war, for the next five or six weeks we were escorting convoys to Greece and Crete and sometimes to Port Said and along the desert coast. Our reduced speed did not matter as it was always slow convoys — old ships that should have been scrapped years before.

There was a lot of airborne activity but sometimes our most unfriendly adversary was the sea which could become rather stormy at that time of year and not very kind to our patched-up bows. This meant that we could be forced to heave to or go stern first if the sea was very rough.

The Desert Army, under the command of General Wavell with R.N. support along the coast was still chasing away Mussolini's Mirages but the introduction of the German Air Force brought disaster to the Allies. Flieger Korps X seemed to have an inexhaustible supply of long and short-range dive-bombers. Their production rate must have been far away greater than ours. Of course, their workers were not allowed to go on strike.

Malta was now completely besieged and all our shipping and defence positions in this part of the world seemed to be well within the range of the Huns. They found it easy to lay magnetic mines in the Suez Canal which proved to be a great menace until the navy came up with the idea of laying nets across the bottom of the Canal at the narrows which enabled them to gently lift the mines to the surface after a raid and then render them harmless.

People talked then, as they do now, about 'making them safe' or 'rendering them harmless' as if it were a routine job just like writing out a request, but to my way of thinking it was a task for none but the really courageous. To the men in the mine and bomb disposal squad it was all in a day's work but it was a very dangerous office and the men had a short life expectancy. I knew two leading torpedo men who left the ship for mine disposal duties and lost their lives within a few months. I noticed it always seemed to be the quiet mild-mannered men who undertook the most hazardous occupations.

When the efficient, highly-trained, ruthless German forces took over the Mediterranean war at the beginning of 1941, we knew we were in for a hard time. At this stage in hostilities the Eastern Mediterranean Fleet led by Admiral Cunningham had no operative aircraft carrier and there were hardly any land based fighter aircraft. Such aircraft as we had were sent to bases in Greece and Crete along with a large force out of our Desert army much against the wiser judgement of General Wavell who was later sacked for being proved right — a typical petty and stupid move by the backroom (or should it be backward?) boys. The Desert Army lads — particularly the Aussies — had a lot of faith in the experienced general and were not happy after he left.

In mid-February we were sent to help with the air defence of Benghazi — still in British hands after the rout of the Italian forces. With four corvettes we escorted a slow convoy including the monitor *H.M.S. Terror* and we gathered in a small petrol tanker on the way.

The crews of these tankers and ammunition ships must have been among the bravest men in the Merchant Navy. One small bomb or torpedo or even an accident could see them all blown into the next world. Sometimes it would be our duty to protect them in convoy and we nearly fouled our breeches if they came too close to us.

With nothing to hinder them the enemy had laid mines all along the desert coast and our accompanying corvettes kept blowing them up just ahead of us, while the sturdy old *H.M.S. Terror* just rolled blissfully over them. It was a bit disconcerting for us. We felt almost naked without any bows from which to stream paravanes and would be helpless in the middle of a minefield by ourselves. But we just had to take our chance and it was amazing how often we got away with it.

We crept into Benghazi, which we soon re-named 'Benghastly'. We had to scrape between wrecks while bombers and mine-laying aircraft attacked us all the time. I was told to take my forward supply party on to the forecastle to help moor the ship alongside the jetty. We had never done anything like this before and none of us was a seaman. We knew very little about knots and splices but as all the real sailors were otherwise engaged firing guns at dive-bombers somebody had to do the job, so it was up to us. We might have been there yet if the shock waves from an underwater explosion had not given us a kindly shove in the right direction at a critical moment.

It was the same experience for the other odds and sods who were sent to make up the mooring party astern. Somebody said something about 'shot and shell'. Old Jack retorted, 'You mean shit and glory'. Once we were safely tied up we had to get along to our action stations as quickly as we could because the guns were needing ammunition.

Formations of high-level and dive-bombers repeatedly attacked all afternoon despite a continuous barrage put up by our own high-angle and close-range guns together with those of all the other ships in the harbour. There were plenty of near misses but no direct hits and a few of our attackers seemed to be damaged by our fire although we did not see any of them come down. A very dark moonless night kept the bombers away later on but we had no rest because mines kept exploding all around us.

Mass attacks started again at dawn and it was impossible to unload the store ships so it was decided that we should return to Tobruk and try to discharge them there. It suited us — we were glad to leave such an unfriendly town.

As we steamed out with all guns blazing the corvette ahead of us picked up the two-man crew of a crashed bomber. The German airmen apparently recognised us from last year's action in Narvik and those arrogant Huns told their rescuers to inform us that we should not be allowed to escape the next time. The Krauts have no sense of humour. I don't know what we had done to annoy the poor souls but we raised our glasses to them in the Fleet Club when we got back and hoped that they would have a lousy time as prisoners of war. And bad luck to them all — they started it.

We left the old monitor *H.M.S. Terror* behind us in Benghazi. We could not help feeling that we had deserted her and left her to her fate, especially when she was still shooting them down as we moved out.

We reached Tobruk and delivered the store ships safely into harbour but there were many attacks on the way. Dive-bombers sank several ships along the coast including three minesweepers and two destroyers as well as causing damage and casualties to a hospital ship which would, no doubt, have given the young Nazi thugs great pleasure. There was nothing they liked more than somebody who could not hit back. That is why we called them 'Nasties'.

H.M.S. Terror eventually fought her way out of Benghazi exploding mines all around her as she went which caused her more flooding. She got as far as Derna before her old hull crumbled under the repeated merciless attacks by dive-bombers. It took a lot of work by the Luftwaffe to put her under and every one of her ship's company upheld the tradition of the old British sea dogs from the time of Alfred the Great.

When we arrived back in Alexandria we had to spend a few hours in the dry dock for a check-up and some repairs to our bow. Then we left harbour again with a slow convoy to Piraeus in company with *H.M.S. Calcutta*. Just two days after leaving harbour we ran smack into a force 8 gale and we had to turn back leaving *Calcutta* to carry on with the convoy. She weathered the storm but her upper deck was cleared of most of its deck fittings and she suffered a real battering which we ourselves would never have survived.

At the beginning of March a big effort was made to bolster the Greek army and a large force of soldiers and equipment, including tanks, had to be transferred as quickly as possible from Egypt to Greece and Crete. Another sister anti-aircraft cruiser — *H.M.S. Carlisle* — joined up with us although she too was in need of repair and was running on one screw. Between us we covered three convoys a week, sometimes together, but more often meeting each other going in and out.

By now there were goodness knows how many Stukas and J.U. 88s based on the island of Rhodes so that we were frequently under attack and a slow convoy going through the Kaso Strait was an easy target. We kept beating off the attacks and shepherded all the ships through safely. It was not getting any easier although it was still not as tough as Narvik.

During one of the March convoys we were again in trouble with the elements. Our patched-up bows started to groan and protest as we struggled with a stormy sea. We nearly went on the rocks when we missed the entrance to Suda Bay but our good captain managed to bring the ship around enough for us to fumble our way into the harbour.

By chance, one of the destroyers in the bay which was flashing up ready to steam to our rescue had among the crew my older brother Jack. I had not seen him for a long time though we had often been on ships which had passed in the night.

Once in a while we would be in Piraeus for long enough to give shore leave into Athens but it always seemed to be Port Watch who were free to take advantage. Some of us in the Starboard Watch were beginning to wonder if we should ever be privileged to enter the ancient city and gaze on the beauty of all its old stones and things. One day we were unexpectedly detained in the Greek port and sailing was postponed until evening. Leave was piped for Starboard Watch from ten hundred hours until fourteen hundred hours.

Dear old 'Jimmy the One' had all the liberty men fall in and told them he was giving them a chance to see the Acropolis or anything else that came to mind but leave was 'till fourteen hundred only', adding sternly, 'I don't care if you come off in a handcart but you must be on board by fourteen hundred'.

There seemed to be no beer in Athens but there was a surplus of champagne. In one establishment, which before the war had been a posh night club owned and managed by an English exile, but which was now a rather seedy drinking den with an equally seedy owner, we just sat and drank the 'society bubbly' out of pint mugs. It could be quite potent and had weird and wonderful effects on the less experienced young sailors, and a few of the older ones too!

At ten minutes before the clock struck two there were still men adrift and the First Lieutenant was furious. We were about to be visited by some very important people and the piping party and all the ship's officers, dressed in their Sunday best were gathered by the gangway. The First Lieutenant in a voice filled with hurt and despair was heard to exclaim, 'I did not believe that my men would let me down', or something like that. Suddenly there were sounds of revelry from afar and into full view came a glorious parade. It was a handcart full of mortally inebriated sailors with a chief petty officer ordnance artificer sitting on top of them playing a mutinous mouth organ. At each corner of the cart pushing and pulling were a sailor and a Royal Marine having changed caps with each other as was the custom when full of the enchanting nectar. The remainder of the jolly Jack-me-Hearties were staggering in 'admiralty sweeps' around the stately conveyance.

The liberty men came to a disorderly halt at the gangway and did their best to stand to attention while respectfully performing the 'off caps' salute. Ratings aboard the ship cheered encouragement and even some of the officers started to laugh but were frozen into silence by a withering look from Number One. With true naval precision the ship's crane was swung outboard carrying a cargo net into which the contents of the handcart were tipped like a haul of fish, hoisted aboard and unceremoniously crammed down a hatch while the Master-at-Arms chased the rest of the party up the gangway and hurried them below decks just a moment before the waiting Rolls Royce limousines pulled up alongside and the Lordly Ones in all their glory with their scrambled eggs and fruit salad and all the rest of it were piped aboard.

After the ball was over the still angry First Lieutenant was deliberating what sort of drastic punishment to impose when it was tactfully pointed out to him that the men **had** actually come back on time and he **had** told them they could come off in a **handcart**. Eventually he saw the funny side of it and let them off with a 'caution' especially after one of the old hands told him he had been saving it up for ages and he didn't mean money.

Such distractions helped to keep up our spirits while we were doing a job which was beginning to get wearisome. It was the same routine day in day out — leave harbour, pick up very slow convoy, attack by Stukas, push the ships along as fast as they would go, probably seven or eight knots through the Kaso Strait, more dive-bombers. Next day, enter Piraeus, unload ships, all night bombing, leave Piraeus for Suda Bay, more air attack, leave Crete, pick up slow convoy of empty ships, more dive-bombers and high-level attacks, reach Alexandria, refuel and ammunition, more air raids — Heaven help the sailors on a night like this!

Mind you, nobody ever needed a laxative. I heard one Royal Marine expounding the wisdom, 'There are two factors which bring officers and men to the same level — bombs and venereal disease!'

The operation to establish an army in Greece carried on until the end of April. In seven weeks the three anti-aircraft cruisers — all in need of repair — had shepherded about seventy thousand British and Anzac troops and their equipment from Egypt to Greece and Crete without loss. Nobody told us at the time that 'those upstairs' were already planning to bring them out.

Another memorable day's work happened near the end of March 1941. After leaving Piraeus we went into Suda Bay, tied up to the oil tanker *Pericles* about midnight, and filled up our fuel tanks. We were ready for sea just before dawn and had, in fact, started to slip when the forecastle party made out the dark shape of a small motor boat speeding towards us. It was assumed to be a duty boat coming out with a last minute order. The boatswain yelled, 'Look out, you stupid bugger. You're going to hit us', and the small craft went right under where our bows used to be and hit the oiler amidships, exploding like a torpedo. At the same time, another of these unidentified missiles crippled the cruiser *H.M.S. York* while a third one landed harmlessly on the beach.

There was pandemonium in the harbour. Nobody could see what was going on and some ships were shooting at imaginary bombers. We went very quickly to action stations and carried on out of harbour as fast as we could to where we had a convoy waiting. All we knew was that if our bows had not been blown off earlier they would have taken the full impact of the explosion instead of the oil tanker *Pericles* which, like the cruiser *York*, was now a wreck. It looked like being one of those days.

Outside Suda Bay we took charge of a rather large convoy of slow empty ships, mostly British or Greek with one or two Egyptians that had managed to get in on the act. Two destroyers had shepherded them from Piraeus but they were now the charge of a small corvette which was trying — like a sheepdog — to keep them in some sort of order. We crashed on at the full speed of the slowest ship which was about ten knots through the dreaded Kaso Strait bound for Port Said and Alexandria.

We expected a few irritations and were not disappointed. First came the usual shadowing Dornier — out of range but we fired a few rounds in his direction just for the hell of it. During the forenoon we drove off several small groups of aircraft who attacked the convoy but did not seem keen to come too close, and we were able to relax for an hour or so, but we stayed at action stations.

Then, in the middle of the afternoon they came, and they came and we thought they were never going to stop coming. It was an awesome picture, like a black cloud of locusts about to descend on a helpless crop, a swarm of about three dozen J.U.88's — one for each ship in the convoy and two for us, hell-bent on pulverising the lot of us.

Keeping watch for his signal I saw the gunner's mate — I could not hear him but his mouth was open — pointing to the heavens so I started running with the ammunition just as all the four-inch guns opened fire with an ear-bashing explosion. They were shooting at such a rate that it was a wonder the barrels did not melt. I thought some of us were going to melt too.

Soon the pom-pom and the point-fives opened up while the corvette and every ship in the convoy which could produce a machine-gun or a handgun, even a few Very pistols, joined the party. The battle seemed to be going on forever but it really lasted for only just over an hour. Doesn't time fly when you're having fun? From our combined effort we thought we had brought down two of the bombers but we could not be sure. Our wireless operators picked up several calls for help.

For all the stramash, the bombers only managed to damage slightly two of the merchant ships and there were no casualties. That was probably our finest hour!

The remainder of the journey was uneventful and twenty-four hours later we were back 'home'. As we steamed into Alexandria all the ships we passed gave us a resounding cheer. It had been quite a trip for them, too — but it's nice to be nice!

The Merchant Navy including the fishing fleet had a very hard life in both peace and war. They were grossly underpaid and their living conditions at sea left a lot to be desired. For generations British merchant seamen proved themselves to be the best in the world. Many of them came from the Highlands and Islands while most of the others, particularly ship's engineers, hailed from the dockyards of the Clyde, Humber, Mersey, and Tyne. They were the real sailors and the backbone of their country. Theirs was probably the most hazardous of any peacetime profession and their experience of injury and loss of life was greater than that of any other industry — even the coal mines.

In wartime many of the fishing boats were commandeered by the Admiralty along with skipper and crew and converted to minesweepers. The boats became warships and their crews were made Royal Naval Reserve personnel with appropriate rank or rating. Some of the bigger trawlers were also fitted with submarine detecting equipment and took part in long-range escort duties including Russian convoys. Former cruise liners were made into armed merchant cruisers and fought with great distinction against powerful German warships.

It was the Merchant Navy who fought the long running Battle of Britain, keeping the country supplied with food and fighting equipment whatever the odds against them. They were civilians but they were in the front line of the fighting. Of course, whatever their grievances they could never 'down tools' and it must have irked them at times when they fought their ships full of urgently needed cargo halfway around the world only to see them lying unattended in a British harbour because of a state of strike by dockers who were far better paid than themselves and had a nice warm bed to go home to at night.

In the early days of the war, most of the merchantmen were unarmed and depended entirely on their escorting warships for protection, although many of them sailed alone. Later on, when they were given the guns these civilian sailors fought with as much zeal and discipline as the men in the armed services who had been trained for the job.

One early example was the small cargo-passenger ship sailing from Shetland coming into harbour with her poop deck adorned by the fuselage of a German bomber which had been brought down by the marksmanship of a ship's steward. The Merchant Navy men did not get much credit for their efforts but they expected none. It was their way of life.

When we got back to Alexandria we found the harbour empty. Our sister ack-ack ships *Calcutta* and *Carlisle* were engaged in convoying ships in and out of Greece and Crete while the battle fleet led by Admiral Cunningham was busy shooting it out with the Italian navy at Cape Matapan.

Next day, our good Captain, in his wisdom kindly promoted me to the rating of supply petty officer (temporary). I have doubts as to whether this sparkling item of information would be very likely to go down in the annals of history as one of the earth shattering events in the song and saga of nautical evolution, but I just thought I should mention it — since nobody else will!

At the beginning of April a night raid by a very large force of German and Italian bombers attacked the Gulf of Athens dropping flares to light up the harbour followed by hundreds of high explosive bombs, sea mines and landmines. Ammunition ships blew up scattering fireballs for quite a distance around them. Most of the nearby laden or empty ships blew up or sank. Many civilians and service personnel lost their lives in the devastation and the Port of Athens which was the only suitable harbour for servicing the war in Greece was reduced to a heap of rubble.

Three cruisers including *Calcutta* with their decks ablaze from flying debris and with their boats all smashed inched their way out of harbour through a deadly hazard of free floating mines, and headed for Suda Bay.

We were ready to go into Piraeus with a convoy of troop reinforcements when we met our old mate *Calcutta* coming out looking as if she had been in a nasty accident and we knew that we were not going to be guzzling champagne in Athens this night. We anchored in the Salamis Strait — scene of a famous naval battle about two-and-a-half thousand years ago (before we came to Greece) and sent half of the convoy into Salamis harbour and the other ships to Volos. We stayed hove-to for two days and then went back to Suda Bay.

Our next mission was to steam north from Crete with a troopship and two destroyers to one of the islands to bring out a British regiment which was in danger of being wiped out by aircraft from German and Italian airfields a few miles away. On a still, fortunately dark, night a fleet of small boats lifted all the soldiers and transferred them to the troopship while we stood at action stations all the time but were not attacked. At dawn, with all the men and their equipment safely lifted off we headed for Alexandria.

It was the middle of April and the evacuation had already begun before our elders and betters announced the end of 'Operation Lustre' planned to reinforce the Greek war front.

Back in Alexandria we refuelled and took on board essential stores and ammunition. One watch had the night ashore while the rest of us passed the time trying to discourage high-level bombers. The next day we slipped out on another mystery tour.

We were destined to make a number of voyages into the unknown from now on. Out we went, sometimes with a convoy, sometimes on our own. Sometimes there would be dive-bombers all over the place, other times we came back without meeting a soul. Occasionally we would hear a buzz about where we had been and what had been done, or we might even read about it in the papers. There was so much propaganda pushed around by 'Lord Haw-Haw' and company that we were told to pay no attention to any news report unless it came from Richard Dimbleby.

One day when an official motor launch approached and its coxswain shouted the appropriate question, 'What ship?' he received the very unorthodox reply from our man on the gangway, 'Damned if I know mate — I only work here'.

We steamed out that morning and picked up our 'flock' which turned out to be two large assault vessels; they were modern, fairly fast former cargo-passenger ships which had been specially strengthened and fitted with anti-aircraft guns. From their davits, instead of the usual lifeboats, hung small landing craft. These ships flew the White Ensign.

We travelled west along the desert coast, closer inshore than fancied, what with mines and things, went somewhere and hung around until dawn then went somewhere else for a couple of days, picked up a few ships and turned for home. During the night, which luckily for us was very dark, our R.D.F. detected a large formation of enemy aircraft approaching and we were ordered to 'quieten ship'. We were closed-up at action stations all night and we could actually hear the enemy overhead as we crawled along, speaking in whispers and making no unnecessary sound or movement, hoping that those above could not hear us or see our wake. It was obvious whom they were searching for. We crossed our fingers, toes and everything and prayed that no ship's funnel would show any sparks and that no tensed up member of one of the merchant ships chose the wrong moment to touch the trigger of a machine-gun. If we had been detected, it would have been curtains for the lot of us. Talk about 'tiptoe through the tulips'.

Eventually they gave up the search and returned to base. Our knotted stomach muscles gradually relaxed and a few chaps raced for the heads as we cracked on speed and got to hell out of it.

Later we heard several stories as to where we had been. One rumour said that we had set out to kidnap some General while another that we had covered a useless raid on Bardia as a sop to the chinless wonders in Whitehall who wanted us to invade and conquer the heavily fortified island of Pantelleria. Whatever it was we were sent out to do, it put at risk a lot of ships and men who were going to be desperately needed in our attempt to rescue a large part of our army now trapped in Southern Greece. We got back to Alexandria the next day, took on stores and ammunition and lay at our friendly mole all night under sailing orders for who knows where.

We steamed out next day at the crack of dawn leaving our Captain ashore in hospital. He had been ill for some time but, like his ship, he could not be spared until he was no longer able to carry on. Outside the harbour we joined up with a destroyer and two troop transport ships. It was a cold, breezy day with enough sea swell to give us an uncomfortable roll but not enough to threaten our shaky bows. Shortly after breakfast we were ordered to 'clear lower deck' and as we stood to attention in the waists, all eyes were on the lower bridge where the First Lieutenant staged his entrance — a tall figure of a man dashingly attired like the commodore of an ancient and worthy yacht club in white drill trousers, black uniform jacket, white ruffed scarf, and white topped cap set at a rakish angle. He stood erect, feet planted firmly on the gently heaving deck, hands tucked imperiously in his jacket pockets waiting for the right moment to begin his oration. For some reason he reminded me of one of those old rams we had seen at Sullom Voe.

Then he spoke! He told us that 'Operation Demon', the battle to take our army out of Greece, was about to commence and that we were on our way to pick up six thousand Australian soldiers including some wounded men who had fought their way to the beaches. He added proudly, 'And I am taking you!'

Yo, ho, ho, up with the Jolly Roger boys and pass the mustard! Bless me feyther's drawers and chase a Chinaman!

There was an affectionate and ironic cheer from the assembled hands. He was a silly old fart but the lads had a lot of confidence in him and would follow wherever he led. There was never that kind of faith in the ship's command again after he left us.

Having heard the prophesy of doom I anticipated the requirement of loads of tea and sandwiches so I started making plans while we had a moment's respite. The first thing to do was to make sure that we had plenty of everything handy in the ship's victualling office which was also the issue room for the daily rations. We needed a good stock of corned beef, evaporated milk, sugar and tea. The bakers were told to double their output of loaves for a day or two. While 'Tanky' was lugging the cases of stuff up from the stores I decided to help by filling up the sugar and tea bins. I was scooping the tea from the packing case to the bin when the ship gave a hard turn and I drove the rusty metal angle on the tea chest deep into my right forearm. When I pulled clear I had to stop the blood from spouting all over the place so I stuck my not very clean thumb over the tear and went to the sickbay as soon as I could get somebody to hold the fort.

The ship carried two medical officers who, of course, always disagreed with each other. They were a Surgeon Commander R.N.V.R. and a regular service Surgeon Lieutenant. The senior doctor was a friendly old chap and as my action station was outside the sickbay we had many a conversation on the subject of first aid. In civilian life he practised as a doctor in a lunatic asylum and told us about the inmates who had escaped, posing as doctors. Sometimes we wondered about him! He was referred to as 'The Witch Doctor' which made it easy for someone to ask, 'Which doctor?' When he saw me using my thumb as a tourniquet he gave me a long lecture on first aid then told me I had done the right thing. Eventually the younger surgeon told me to sit down while he cleaned the wound and put in a few stitches. The needlework did not last for long as we were in action a few hours later and I had to use my right arm, but that was the nearest thing I ever suffered to a 'war wound'. I was one of the 'Buckie luggers'.

On our first day at sea the enemy left us alone except for the usual shadowing Dornier which eventually flew high overhead and dropped a couple of bombs which were not close enough to do us any harm. The next afternoon the defence watch had already opened fire when we scrambled to action stations as bombs were falling all around us. One of the transports — a Dutchman — was hit and set on fire. We were on a tight schedule and had to speed on leaving the trooper with the destroyer in company. She was attacked again later and sank; the destroyer picked up her surviving crew. To take her place three destroyers were sent from Suda Bay. We should have been issued with shoehorns because it was going to be a very tight fit to pack all those soldiers into such space as we had among us.

Once again we had the good fortune of a very dark night as we stole cautiously into the bay. We felt sure that we had not been spotted but the rattle of the anchor chains and the lowering of boats seemed to shriek out in the stillness and we were convinced that we would be heard miles away. Then we saw the flashes of explosives on the beach as the Aussies started to blow up their artillery and vehicles, destroying everything that they could not carry with them. All the ships sent in every available craft including motor boats towing whalers and by dawn we had lifted off all the soldiers and nurses we could find and were on our way. We ourselves took on board about twelve hundred men and as soon as they arrived we gave them a large cup of tea and a handful of sandwiches and herded them onto the mess decks. One chap was seen to drink thirteen cups of tea before he fell asleep.

They were all smartly turned out and did not seem to be the least bit harassed. They had taken it for granted that the navy would come for them. Some of them had even donned new uniforms before disposing of their old outfits. When they were really up against it these rough, tough, hard-drinking, fun-loving, friendly Australians had a brave quiet discipline which they managed without all the 'ballshine' so beloved of other armies.

We had gone unmolested through the night for which we were very thankful but soon after we got underway again we were spotted and attacked by about a dozen Heinkel bombers who came straight for us. The ploy of the Luftwaffe had changed and it now seemed that they thought it best to destroy the escorts first, leaving the convoy at their mercy. Of course, we did not go along with that idea and they found us very unco-operative. Our barrage kept the first wave too high for accurate bombing and by the time the next lot came with a more determined attack every Australian soldier was on the upper deck firing his rifle or machine-gun. We noticed one soldier resting the barrel of his anti-tank gun on the shoulder of his mate pumping away for dear life. I think the sheer audacity of it all would have been enough to discourage most of the attackers.

We were getting to the stage where some of the gun linings were badly worn and we had a few premature bursts which sprayed the gun deck with shrapnel, wounding one petty officer.

We reached Crete about noon passing *Calcutta* on her way in for a second load. Going into Suda Bay we were attacked by a sizeable force of J.U. 88s which we managed to fight off and then to the astonishment of all of us and encouraging shouts from the Aussies a flight of British fighter planes appeared from somewhere and got stuck into the Huns, shooting two or three of them down and driving the others away. We landed our passengers at Suda Bay to many cheers and shouts of thanks.

As soon as the decks were cleared we hurried out to join forces with *Calcutta* in the gulf where she and her convoys were packed with soldiers. Some of the ships had taken on too many passengers for their own safety and the men had to be taken off and transferred to other vessels.

In a rough sea while under airborne attack, this is not an exercise to be recommended and I am sure it was not then in the seamanship manual, but it was managed without loss, for which many a prayer was offered. Others involved in this evacuation force did not get away with it. One troop carrier and two destroyers, together with many soldiers and sailors had gone down before we joined up with them. Then in the afternoon we came across a cruiser taking off a thousand men from a sinking Dutch transport. We all sailed on together, decks crowded with men and after succeeding in driving off three more attacks we arrived safely in Alexandria where we spent the night changing the worn-out gun linings amidst continuous bombing.

The evacuation from Greece ended when our other sister ack-ack ship *H.M.S. Carlisle* with her two destroyers lifted the patiently waiting rearguard of two-and-a-half thousand New Zealand soldiers from the beach and steamed as fast as they could in a fairly rough sea to Suda Bay. Altogether over fifty thousand service men and women who should never have been sent there in the first place had been safely evacuated but at least a thousand helpless soldiers had been lost at sea along with many sailors who were trying to save them. The poor old infantry, as usual, had to take another hammering.

Later, the First Lieutenant, not as exultant as he had been a few days ago, cleared lower deck and thanked us for doing a good day's work and all the rest of it. He had not done so badly himself as Skipper either. He told us that two decorations had been awarded to the ship — a Distinguished Service Cross for an officer and a Distinguished Service Medal for a rating. He said he could not recommend any man more than another so the name would be drawn out of a hat. Fair enough if **all** the names had gone into the hat in the first place, but that was the way they did things.

It was now the end of April and the fleet had taken a few hard knocks but there was far worse to come.

At the beginning of May it was decided to send a large heavily armed convoy from both east and west to supply and reinforce Malta and to bring through more ships for Admiral Cunningham's Eastern Mediterranean Fleet. This looked like a near impossible task with the German and Italian air forces having almost complete control of the skies. But fate smiled on us this time and gave us unusually poor weather with a very low ceiling which kept the bombers away most of the time. Whenever we were attacked the guns from our three anti-aircraft ships together with the far more effective weapons of the three new Dido class cruisers proved too much for them.

By the middle of May it became well known that the Germans had constructed new airfields all over Greece and the islands of the Aegean and that they had at least a thousand bombers and fighters in readiness, as well as hundreds of transport planes and gliders all within striking distance of Crete. It was obvious to everybody here, even the bug Arabs, but clearly of no significance to the ruling barons in their ivory dugouts, that friend Adolph was ready to give the order to pour into the hopelessly under-fortified island. We all knew it could not possibly hold out for very long in the face of all that the German forces could throw against it.

Still, it was our duty to defend the place as best we could and, with this in mind, most of the Eastern Mediterranean Fleet deployed south and west of Crete ready to move north as soon as the fun started. Of course, we had no fighter protection. We joined up with Force C comprising four destroyers with the light cruiser *H.M.S. Dido* as flagship and we patrolled all around the east coast of Crete looking for invasion forces. We were closed-up at full action stations night and day and were repeatedly attacked by high-level and dive-bombers with a few torpedo carrying aircraft to add a bit of spice to the proceedings. The weather was starting to become hot and it was not very comfortable, especially below decks. Being unable to strip for a wash did not make things any better.

About a week later we had to return to Alexandria to fit new gun linings and take on fuel, stores and ammunition. All night leave was given to part of the watch. I went ashore for the first time in three months but it did not do me much good. At about ten o'clock at night messages were flashed in cinemas, the Fleet Club, bars and anywhere that it was thought sailors might be found while patrols were sent ashore to chase everybody back to the ship. Most of us made our way back as quickly as we could but there were some who seemed to have disappeared from the face of the earth.

When I got back aboard I saw the food and provisions — my responsibility — being loaded and stored without anybody taking count. This was sacrilege! How could I possibly explain this unthinkable digression from the laid-down procedure so dear to the hearts of those omnipotent civil servants to whom the pen was always mightier than the Plimsoll line?

Dawn was coming up as we steamed out of harbour and made all the speed we could for the Kaso Strait where a call for help had come from a hospital ship which was being molested by enemy aircraft. Attacking helpless targets was a popular sport among the young Nazis as many a column of refugees could confirm. Several hospital ships had been attacked and sunk already. There was no excuse for this — these vessels were unarmed and clearly marked.

With part of our ship's company left behind in Alexandria we were short of two gun crews and some of the engineroom staff so that we were not in the best state of defence above or below decks and when the Stukas turned their attention on us two of them managed to get through our barrage close enough to near miss the ship with their bombs and spray the decks with machine-gunfire.

When we finally drove the barbarians away and had time to look around it was not a pretty sight. There were a few badly wounded men and some less seriously hurt. One poor chap died later despite heroic work by the surgeon and the sickbay staff. A Royal Marine was badly burned when he smothered a blazing shell case with his body but he survived the ordeal and, like all the others, he carried on with his duties until the action was over. There were quite a few acts of courage and unselfishness, most of which went unreported.

Once it was considered safe to leave the hospital ship we headed back to Alexandria, stopping on the way to bury at sea a good and well-liked shipmate. A few months later we learned that the action had been considered a good propaganda exercise and had earned quite a few decorations including three of the highest awards being a Victoria Cross (posthumous) a Conspicuous Gallantry Medal and a Distinguished Service Order. Several Distinguished Service Medals were awarded and quite a few Mentions in Dispatches including one or two for men who were not even on the ship at the time.

Sadly, there were also two stokers who could not cope with the situation, being down in the boiler-room hearing the fearful thumps of near miss explosions getting closer and closer, knowing that they had a good chance of being boiled alive if the ship was hit, their nerves finally cracked and they left their duties and ran to the upper deck. They were charged with deserting their post and sentenced to a long spell in prison.

I often wonder what I would have done had I been in their shoes. I served most of the war at sea subsequently on a frigate in the North Atlantic then on an aircraft carrier in the Pacific Ocean but not once was I called upon to perform a brave deed. I shall never know whether I would have been a hero or a coward. Certainly I did not feel very courageous so it was just as well that I was never put to the test. Wise old Jack remarked, 'Sometimes it takes more courage to be a coward'.

We tied up in Alexandria the next morning and spent the day repairing the worn-out guns, transferring the wounded to hospital and taking on replacements including a new captain — actually he was only a Commander but he was senior to 'Old Rumple' who had to go back to being First Lieutenant.

We had some laughs with the wounded lads on the way back to port. One young blonde, blue-eyed able seaman was hanging on to the bullet which had shot him, as he said to a few old-timers, 'Up the "A" bracket where you would like to have been'. A petty officer who had also been wounded in a sensitive place was hoping that he would not find himself in the hands of a good-looking nurse because he dreaded the thought of getting over excited.

It was an even better laugh when one of the men who came to replace the wounded answered to the name of 'Newdick'.

After a hard day's work getting shipshape again we left Alexandria escorting an assault ship to land reinforcements on the southern coast of Crete. We got through unscathed and were back in harbour two days later where the ship filled up again and sailed with more soldiers for the same place. This time we did not get away with it. First came dive-bombing and strafing attacks by a number of Stukas. All their bombs missed but the assault ship's landing craft on their davits were wrecked by bullets. Then we faced the J.U.88's with torpedoes. Both the Germans and Italians were good at this kind of warfare using first class, new aircraft for their work while the Royal Navy who invented the game were still having to make do with the old string-back biplanes which succeeded only because of the skill and courage of the men who flew them. It was not until later in the war when we acquired American designed and made, purpose built carrier aircraft that our ships' air-crews had the opportunity to really prove that they had the capability to match the courage with which they were born.

We managed to fight off all the attacks but we were now sure that we could not land the troops safely before dawn so the Big Boss told us to go away home.

Just then we received news that the mighty battle cruiser *H.M.S. Hood*, pride of the Royal Navy, had been sunk by one salvo from the new German battleship *Bismarck* and **that** did not exactly raise our drooping spirits. It also meant the operation to find and sink this very efficient German battleship required the services of half the British navy including warships and aircraft badly needed in the Eastern Mediterranean. We had already lost two heavy cruisers.

In due course the message managed to get through to those befuddled brains back home that it was not good form to keep throwing away ships and lives just for the ancient glory of it all so permission was finally given to get our boys out of Crete as soon as possible and another evacuation officially began.

We left Alexandria during the first watch along with *Calcutta* to join the squadron of cruisers, destroyers and transports with orders to bring out a large number of men from the beaches. We arrived there without much bother and the rest of the squadron went in as close to the beach as they could get while we two flak ships patrolled out to seaward hoping to deal with any surprise attacks from torpedo-bombers. By half-past-three in the morning the ships had lifted off nearly six thousand patiently waiting soldiers and we turned for the home run. We were just passing around 'breakfast' to the ship's company at their action stations, where they had been all night, when the attacks started. We and *Calcutta* closed in on either side of the troopship and put up the best barrage we could make against the dive-bombers and drove them away. They attacked again an hour later and scored a hit on the Australian cruiser but she kept going. A third attack at noon near missed a cruiser and a destroyer but so far we had kept the trooper safe. We did not shoot any down but must have given some of them a headache.

As we came near to Alexandria what we thought was a mirage turned out to be two of our own R.A.F. fighter planes from a desert airfield and we went safely into harbour with a lot of not too unhappy soldiers. We tied up around midnight in the middle of a heavy air raid. The bombing lasted right through the middle watch then allowed half the watch to get a couple of hours' rest before our enthusiastic drummer sounded 'Charlie, Charlie'.

It was Saturday, the last day of May 1941.

Dog tired though we were there was plenty of work to be done that forenoon by everybody except four of the R.N.V.R. lads who had received draft chits home to be turned into Sub Lieutenants. There were also two other bomb-happy ratings sent to hospital. We had to load up again with fuel and ammunition and provisions, and required more of the guns relined; they were wearing out quickly with the continuous firing.

After a few hours' rest we steamed out and piled on as many knots as our bow repairs would allow. This time we were led by *Calcutta*. Our orders were to meet up with another convoy of ships full of soldiers lifted off the beaches who had reported being under frequent attack and in need of help.

It seemed such a peaceful morning as if the war were a long way away as we steamed along on the smooth, deep blue sea feeling like we had not a care in the world. Suddenly our lookouts spotted J.U.88's diving out of the sun and reported bombs falling. Our navigator turned the ship hard-a-starboard and a stick of bombs fell so close to our stern that we nearly turned over. You could hear the sigh of relief throughout the ship.

But *H.M.S. Calcutta's* luck finally deserted her. She received a direct hit which blew her apart and in the blink of an eye she was gone, taking half of her crew with her. We could not believe it.

By tradition, the first ship of the line would be the vessel with the senior Captain. Previously, when *Coventry* and *Calcutta* had sailed together we had always been the leader because ours was the senior ranking Captain, but now our Commanding Officer was junior in rank so *Calcutta* went ahead and it was the leading ship which 'bought it'.

Lady Luck seemed to be still with us! But not with poor old *Calcutta*.

Where this proud little ship had been a few moments ago the sea was awash with alive and dead sailors. These were our mates — especially those who trained with the London R.N.V.R. in the days before the war. For a year-and-a-half we steamed in convoy together and fought off all that the might of the enemy air forces could hurl against us, although *Calcutta* endured a lot more action than we did. We ought to have been prepared for what was to be faced but how could anybody ever be ready for that? We got our whalers in the water and scrambling nets over the side as quickly as could be done, but remained closed-up at action stations expecting the Luftwaffe to return in force to finish us off, which, for some reason they failed to do. We were a sitting target. It seemed to be a long time before we picked up all that were left of *Calcutta's* ship's company. Some were already dead and others did not last much longer — bruised and battered bodies burned, scalded, blackened with oil, arms and legs torn off, gaping wounds and seemingly unharmed men so dazed that they did not know who or where they were. They were the fellows with whom we had boozed and brawled from the North Cape to the Suez Canal.

It was the glorious First of June.

When the survivors were safely on board and the ship secured we headed back for Alexandria with all the speed we could make praying that our forepart would stay together. Fortunately the weather stayed friendly and we came back safely at about three o'clock in the afternoon going straight alongside the survivors' berth at Shed 45 — a very busy place just now

— where ambulances and transports were waiting. As soon as we had discharged our passengers we moved to our normal mooring at C.2 gazing sadly at the empty place astern. An hour or two later we watched the heavily laden ships from Crete whom we had gone out with *Calcutta* to rescue come into the harbour unharmed after what had turned out to be a trouble-free run.

And as far as we were concerned, that was the end of the 'Hellenic House of Horror' — a fruitless expedition that was doomed from the start, as everybody engaged in the operation had always known. The Eastern Mediterranean Fleet had seen most of its warships sunk or badly damaged along with a large number of merchant ships and over two thousand good seamen had perished.

Many soldiers also went down with the ships but at least we did manage to bring back more than half of those we landed there a few months ago. It was an unseemly waste of lives but who, except those who had lost loved ones, cared about that?

It was our second evacuation in six weeks and our fifth since the war started. We were getting to be a removal firm.

To show their appreciation in typical Antipodean fashion the Australian Army donated two flagons of Australian bitter (the best beer you could get away from home) to every man in the British fleet who took part in the evacuation. It was a grand gesture. I wonder who got the chance to drink it? Certainly not many of those who took an active part — half of them were dead.

We remained in Alexandria for four days, enduring the usual nightly air raids, and then we followed the sweepers through a heavily mined harbour entrance and made for Port Said where we tied up to a buoy for the night. We steamed out the next day in the company of two destroyers and an assault ship packed with soldiers of the Black Watch Regiment. Their duty was to land on the Lebanese coast just north of Palestine and capture a bridge ahead of a mixed army of British, Australian, Polish and Free French troops who were fighting the very pro-German Vichy French forces. This proved to be a disaster. As usual, everybody knew all about it in advance — except us. The landing party, once safely ashore, was ambushed and slaughtered by the French Nazis. Meanwhile the Aussies had already crossed the river by pontoon.

The total Royal Navy support for this operation consisted of ourselves, two other damaged light cruisers and a few destroyers and corvettes. We had also managed to scrape together about a dozen R.N. and R.A.F. 'prehistoric' fighter aircraft which helped a little — but not a lot.

The French navy had a flotilla of large, powerful destroyers to support their well-equipped army and airforce under the command of a fanatical French Nazi General. There were a few of those around at the time — until they started losing.

The empty assault craft returned to Port Said and we joined the Admiral and his ships in Haifa. One of our destroyers, patrolling the coast alone, was set upon by two of the powerful Frenchmen, damaged and stopped. Fortunately two of our own boats arrived before the Froggies could move in for the kill, so the enemy showed the usual French discretion and beat it.

In Haifa just as in Alexandria we spent half the night in action against German and Italian aircraft. We suffered a few near misses but little damage, except to our feelings. Some times the bombs fell close enough to shower the deck with stones, mud and all sorts of nasties which did not smell all that pleasant. These foul deeds brought forth many nautical remarks which I am sure did not have their origin in the Seamanship Manual or any other known Bible. They seemed to have something to do with the ancestry of our assailants particularly the legitimacy of their birth and that of their fathers before them. On one occasion, a voice from north of the River Tweed was heard to remark, 'Mud, blood, and shite, the Huns are out tonight'. Another time when somebody said, 'They're really throwing shit at us now'. One of our intellectuals observed, 'There's criticism for you!'

For the next two days we patrolled the Lebanese coast trying to protect our soldiers from the Nazi air forces and their French collaborators. A few Fleet Air Arm Fulmars tried to help but they were no match for the modern French aircraft one of which raked our deck with machine-gun bullets but did not hurt anybody. We returned to Haifa to spend the night under continuous air attack.

Then we steamed up and down the coast of Sidon covering our destroyers who were bombarding French army units. Two of their big boats came around the corner and started lobbing shells in our direction but their salvos fell short. We turned to face them but they did not want to play and decided it was time to go home. They were too fast for us. For a moment it did look as though we might bring them to battle until we found ourselves becoming the target for nasty-minded shore batteries who were bigger than us. We moved further out to sea where we came under attack from Italian bombers based on Crete causing one of the lads to remark, 'We seem to be having to fight every foreign barsteward in this fornicating war.' Bombing attacks continued until dark but we were not hit.

There was a more determined effort next morning by a fairly large formation of J.U. 88s who scored hits on both our accompanying destroyers but they were able to keep going and our combined barrage prevented further damage until we saw them safe in the port of Haifa.

We then carried on to Port Said where we spent the next three nights shooting at enemy aircraft who were trying to block the Suez Canal. While there our experienced Gunnery Officer left us and was replaced by a chap straight out of gunnery school. He would soon learn all about it in our school.

We went back to Haifa and stayed there for a reasonably quiet week trying to learn about modern warfare. The First Lieutenant thought it would be a good idea that the forward supply party — my action group — should be able to act as sea boat's crew in an emergency and gave the order for us to do so there and then. Since neither I nor any of my gang was trained we knew very little about handling sea boats and I, who would have to be the coxswain, knew least of all, so I guess I just had to learn. I scrambled into the boat with an experienced leading seaman and crew, was lowered to the water, shown how to release the boat from the davits, rowed around for a bit, came back to the ship and was shown how to secure the whaler to the blocks ready for lifting. All very exciting. At least I would have some idea what to do if the job was forced on me.

Ah — but yes, there was just one thing! All the strong, fit sailors scrambled up to the top like monkeys, surely expecting me to follow. I looked up. The boat's davits seemed to be at least a mile away up in Heaven drooping slender vines suspended on 'sky-hooks'. I had never learned how to climb ropes and in any case I was a seven stone weakling with biceps about the size of ping-pong balls. There was nothing for me to do but just sit there like an oatmeal monument for how long I did not care to guess. I was beginning to worry because it would soon be time for 'Up Spirits' and I was in charge of the rum issue. I could imagine the stress and strain it would cause if I were late with the 'bubbly'. Eventually 'stand easy' was over, lower deck was cleared, all hands went through the Nelsonian routine of hoisting the long boat and I was returned to the bosom of the ship. I was glad it was only 'for exercise'. I hoped I should never have to do it in earnest.

On Sunday we were back in our old billet in Alexandria. We missed our sister ship who always used to tie up astern, but we would have to get used to it. The show must go on, and most of us were clowns anyway. There seemed to be a sort of post-something depression in Alexandria. The year had started off so well, with the Italians on the run in the desert and the Greeks mopping them up in Albania. Now the Germans had taken over and pushed our desert army right back to El Alamein at the same time as we were being thrown out of Greece and Crete. Half the Eastern

Mediterranean Fleet had been sunk and the remainder of the ships, all but a few of us, had been sent away for major repairs. We watched them leave one by one, battered until they could hardly keep afloat, and those of us here still were not in the best of health. We were all that was left of a once proud and powerful fleet.

To add to the matelots' misery all the 'houses of pleasure' in the Rue de Soeurs — better known as 'Sister Street' — had been razed to the ground by landmines. It must have been the rotten Germans. I am sure the Italians would have been more understanding. We were talking about it in the Fleet Club one night and old Sam remarked that he could never understand a man fancying a woman who looked like Dracula's mother-in-law. Another chap, I think he was an Australian, exclaimed, 'Wouldn't worry me if she'd a face like a hat full of a***holes; you don't look at the mantelpiece when you poke the fire'. Old Ginger sighed, 'Ah well, if I'd been rigged fore and aft there'd have been a whore in our family. I wonder what Lord Haw Haw would have said about that?'

But then came another momentous event which gave us a new lease of life. On 22nd June 1941 German troops invaded Russia as part of Hitler's stated plan to 'liberate' the world. Less than two years before Adolph Hitler and Joe Stalin had been pals and there were still many people who believed in both of them. Now they would have to choose sides. But we on the lower deck were not all that taken up with politics at this particular time — such lofty ideals belonged to the intellectuals. We had a war to fight. What it meant to us was that there would now be somebody else to share the Stukas with us, although for a long time it looked as if there were plenty of those abominations to go around.

The night raids on Alexandria continued without let-up and now that there were fewer ships in the harbour, our four-inch guns had to do a lot more work. The Luftwaffe seemed to be able to unload bombs and landmines at will. Will did not like it either!

The Egyptian residents were naturally becoming a bit demoralised and resentful. After all, the war was not of their making and they were now less well disposed towards the British servicemen. It is fine when you are winning but you don't have many friends when you appear to be on the losing side. Besides which, the shops, bars, the felucca men, and all the other traders had lost a lot of their customers when the fleet left.

We stayed in harbour for nearly three weeks with the watch ashore enjoying night leave while those of us on board spent half the night at action stations as part of the port's defence. We went into Gabari dock for two days so that the shipwrights and engineers could put on a bit more sticking plaster and then we had to take on a load of stores and provisions.

Like most executives our First Lieutenant believed that his role in life was far too important to be bothered with irksome routines such as storing ship and he considered he was doing the supply staff a favour if he condescended to lend them a few of his seamen to help them load their damned food and stuff. That morning he had agreed to let us have a working party after dinner but he forgot all about it and gave the men a make-and-mend afternoon off. When the dockyard lighter came alongside he refused to call out the hands and went away to get his head down. Not to worry. For two or three buckshee cartons of duty-free cigarettes the hard working Egyptian stevedores had the cargo on board and safely stowed in a fraction of the time it would have taken the whole duty watch. When 'Jimmy the One' awoke from his siesta he was not pleased.

Replenishing stocks was always awkward and frustrating when heavy bags, boxes and barrels had to be lowered down through two or three hatches which were barely wide enough for their safe passage. Sometimes the working party would not make a very good job of securing the load which could be hazardous for the poor chap below who often had to be me, and I now have the rheumaticky toes and things to remind me of it. One day the 'chief pusser' asked the 'buffer' to include the tying of the 'barrel sling' in his daily seamanship quiz and it seemed that only the supply ratings knew the proper way to do it. The First Lieutenant did not like that either!

Mid-July we left for Port Said where we picked up a convoy bound for Beirut which was now in Allied hands after all the Nazi French had been driven out. It seemed as if the war had never touched this place. Beirut carried on a normal French Colonial city life; the shops were still well stocked and there was any amount of food and drink and all sorts of exciting things to do. We relieved *H.M.S. Carlisle* as guard ship although there seemed to be nothing to guard. We stayed there for a wonderful three weeks' holiday.

It was a great chance to blow away the cobwebs and get the body toned up again. Some of us obtained the use of a ship's whaler which we pulled across the wide picturesque harbour every morning before breakfast. The clear blue sea was calm and inviting so a mate and I went for a swim as often as we could. We were neither of us very good swimmers but we just concentrated on moving away from the ship and then keeping afloat for half-an-hour at a time which we hoped would be enough to save our skins if ever we had to abandon ship.

Of course the daily duties still had to be carried out and the ship had to keep an action watch which, to everyone's relief, was never called upon to open fire. The First Lieutenant saw to it that life aboard was as easy as possible. Somebody organised coach tours to far away places. The coaches were old Army trucks with wooden planks for seats. Their maniacal Syrian drivers took us, half the time on two wheels, around the cliff-top narrow roads of the town then went tearing across the Plains of Lebanon at a full rate of knots. It seemed to be the custom for our driver to lean out of his window, keeping one hand on the wheel and the other hand waving to the truck driver behind. What they shouted to each other was foreign to our ears but it sounded very rude. We took in the ruins of Baalbek and Byblos and purchased bottles of good wine from the monasteries along the way and then raced back over narrow mountain tracks in the dark.

It was too good to last and by the middle of August we were back on anti-aircraft duty in Port Said, having refuelled at Alexandria on the way. Here we unloaded a cargo of fresh potatoes from Beirut for the navy's victualling stores where they had been keeping the men fed on yams. We stayed in Port Said for a few days while our 'oppo' *H.M.S. Carlisle* guarded the other end of the Suez Canal at Port Taufiq. We were given a few hours' shore leave at night. One night, while waiting for the liberty boat, I was intrigued by an old sailor who was enjoying a drink in a large bar near to the jetty. Every now and then he would stagger out of the bar, lean up against a tree, solemnly take out his false teeth, spew up a bellyful of Egyptian brewed 'Stella' beer, put back in his teeth, and reel back into the bar. He repeated this manoeuvre several times while we were watching.

Another time, the last of the night's liberty boats for chief and petty officers was about to leave the pier when our hard-drinking First Lieutenant stepped aboard. The returning leave party were all in good spirits singing and swearing like any normal well behaved men, which seemed to annoy the not very sober 'Jimmy the One' and he shouted to them to make less noise. Naturally nobody paid a blind bit of notice so he shook one chief petty officer by the shoulder saying, 'I gave you an order, d'ya hear?' The aggrieved man belligerently replied, 'Don't you lay your hands on me, mate, or I'll bloody well thump you in self defence, Sir.' He was about half the size of 'Jimmy' who stood in silence the rest of the trip. When we reached the ship the men dutifully stepped aside to allow him to go first up the gangway and straight to his cabin. Shortly afterwards, a message came for the chief petty officer to report to the First Lieutenant's cabin where, we were told, he found the old fellow sitting morosely at his desk on which there were a service Colt revolver and two large glasses of whisky. He presented the pistol butt first, saying with a heavy voice, 'I have disgraced myself. It is your duty to shoot me.' The chief petty officer replied, 'I'm not going to shoot you.' 'Then have a drink,' and presented him with a large whisky. It was said that they never spoke to each other again.

The following day we took yet another trip through the Canal to Port Taufiq. At this stage it was only the dedication of our shipwrights and engineers which was keeping the ship afloat. *H.M.S. Carlisle* was in much the same sorry state too, but at least her hull was still sound. Here we shared between us the work of escorting ships up and down the Red Sea and the Gulf of Suez. There were warships going away for repairs and others coming back as good as new, and there were troopships and freighters which we escorted up to Port Taufiq, waited while they unloaded, and then took back the empties.

The enemy air forces now had plenty of long-range bombers within easy reach of targets in the Suez Canal and even the Red Sea, so in order to reduce the waiting time and risk in Port Taufiq a resting place was set up in an inlet at the southern end of the Gulf of Suez. This place was given the fitting name of F Anchorage. We were not told what the letter F stood for, but some of us had a good idea of our own. We took turns with *Carlisle* to guard the ships there or take them up to Taufiq then back down the Gulf of Suez and into the Red Sea. It was a 'Bobby's Job', but a hell of a warm one.

F Anchorage felt as if it were right in the middle of the desert. There was hardly any breeze at all and the only thing we could see was sand and more sand. We expected Lawrence of Arabia at any minute. Sometimes, during an air attack, the guns were almost too hot to handle, while as before we had to keep the deck sprayed with sea water, and it was certainly no picnic for the stokers. At my office desk I had to bandage my arms and forehead with blotting paper in a vain effort to stop the sweat dropping on to the accounts I was trying to write, thus washing away the figures. I was glad I was not a chef. There seemed never to be any 'cool of the evening' either.

Someone started a fishing competition during the day watches and at times there were so many lines over the side that the sailors called it 'Margate

Pier'. The trouble was that most of the lads did not know what to do with the fish when they caught them. The only way they had seen fish before was in batter along with a newspaper full of chips.

At the start of October we observed more of the Royal Navy appearing at F Anchorage, muscling in on our activities. There were two modern light cruisers, some Hunt class destroyers and a couple of sloops, all bristling with anti-aircraft guns. A number of large liners filled with troop reinforcements for the army of the Nile was speeding up the Red Sea and would probably demand more protection than the old gash boats would be able to provide. The new arrivals were welcome to the 'Club'.

One day we had just shepherded a pair of Australian troopships into Port Taufiq when we received orders to navigate the Suez Canal once more and steam to Alexandria. We were going through the Bitter Lakes fighting off attacks by J.U.88s when we heard through the amateur bridge report system that a following oil tanker had been blown up by an acoustic mine which we had just passed meekly by. Lucky for us! We spent one night in Alexandria taking on fuel and ammunition and then it was back through the same old canal for a night in Port Taufiq. And what a night it was!

There was a lot of anti-British feeling among the Arabs, manipulated by the German agents who found it easy to roam around freely in Egypt where national security was non-existent, especially now when we had our backs to the wall. Some of our stokers, having a few hours ashore in the town of Suez, were set upon by a gang of Arab thugs. A local police patrol appeared as if to rescue the lads but instead they joined in the attack against the British.

An Army Red Cap patrol arrived, fired a revolver into the air and waited for reinforcements. Eventually the stokers fought their way through the mob but not before one young lad named Stanley had his nose smashed in by an Egyptian policeman's rifle butt and had to be taken to the military hospital.

A few days later a number of Australian soldiers were in Suez — some of the same men to whom we had given a lift out of Greece a few months before. When they heard what had happened to one of their navy friends they just about laid the town flat.

One fine day the Captain cleared lower deck and told us that we should be escorting a convoy to Aden and then, at long last, we were going away for a refit taking about two months.

A dockyard, but where? A home port? South Africa? The U.S.A.? Ah well, no, not exactly. Our happy holiday was to be spent in — wait for it — Bombay! Allee some piccolo player, just our flaming luck.

When we asked the old hands who had been everywhere and seen everything for their opinion of the standard of life and entertainment in Bombay we received the usual answer, 'No proper pubs, lousy beer'. This did not mean very much because many of these time-served men had travelled the world and never ventured any further abroad than the first drinking den outside the dockyard.

Ah well, at least we could get a bit of rest. Bombay was too far away for attack by the German and Italian aircraft and the Japanese were still busy telling us all what a friend we had in Tojo. It could have been worse.

A few weeks before we learned our horoscope I had been aggravated by a persistent cough and I was advised to see the 'quack'. In the sickbay, the two medical officers discussed my case with the junior doctor making a diagnosis which the senior officer overruled in the true Service manner. I was told to get plenty of fresh air and rest and was given a little pill to take there and then. I did not know what the pill contained or what it was meant to do but it certainly produced a bow-wave astern along with everything I had eaten the day before. A few nights later I went ashore for the first time in months and my mates helped me to drown my sorrows. I awoke next morning to find that my cough was gone along with a month's wages, my recently purchased waterproof, shock-proof, dust-proof and everything except thief-proof wrist watch and my new petty officer's cap.

Meanwhile, the medical staff still had me on their books and, when it was known that we were about to journey to less energetic climes, the man with the stethoscope sent for me and told me that I must now keep to the upper deck in the fresh air and must not go near any food distribution until the ship reached Bombay where I could be X-rayed. At the same time I was given a direct order that I was not to imagine that I had developed tuberculosis. I don't know what else I was supposed to think under the circumstances.

TB was a menace throughout the Royal Navy and Merchant Service at that time, especially in older, small ships like this one where we were crammed so close together that the disease could spread like wildfire. It was looked upon by most people as a terminal sickness so I was a wee bit concerned. As usual, old Jack was there with the comforting advice, 'Pay no attention to the "quack". I went to see him about piles. He gave me some dirty great pills which had a hell of a taste and for all the good they did, I might as well have shoved them up me arse'.

The day after we reached Bombay I reported to the military hospital where I was even more worried when the army male nurse seemed to take a long time to manoeuvre my half naked body into the X-ray unit exclaiming, 'Ooh — all you sailors have such lovely big chests!' Fortunately, the other chap with us had a bigger one so he lost interest in me. The examination showed that my lungs were clear and I never did find out what had been wrong with me but I thought it best not to go back to the hospital just in case. The male nurse might have had a friend.

We approached the great, ancient Indian port just before daylight and had been taken aback on seeing the flashing harbour lights all up and down the coast and no sign of blackout in the city. It gave us the feeling that the war and all its horror was somewhere in a different world which we had left far behind us. We moved into dry dock the next day and the ship's company was transferred to living accommodation ashore. The junior ratings up to and including leading hands were billeted in the Army Barracks at Calabar while most of the chiefs and petty officers were housed in two former tourist hotels not far from the dockyard to where we strolled each morning for an easy nine-to-five 'day at the office'.

For the supply staff it was a hectic three or four weeks. All the stores and provisions had to be cleared from the ship for storage in dockyard warehouses after they had been counted, item by item, marked, valued, and recorded. From then on there was little to do except show a presence. It was a glorious waste of time, but no doubt the rest would do us good. We fairly lived it up in the hotels — just two or three to a room and we sat down to three leisurely meals every day waited on by a host of Goanese ship's stewards under the command of a fearsome looking Portuguese major-domo, who saw to it that we were well provided for. And the bugs appeared to enjoy our company as well.

We felt right civilised lying in a real bed between soft cotton sheets and wearing proper night attire instead of sleeping in our underwear. 'Old Dave' told us that when he got married he wore only the top half of his pyjamas but kept the trousers under the pillow in case there was a fire. He said his wife trimmed the hem of her nightgown with fur so that it would keep her neck warm!

Bombay, with all its mystic eastern charm and exotic aromas (one way of putting it) was completely different to any other place most of us had ever visited and it was far away from the war. It took us a while to relax, but gradually we began to take advantage of the scene.

Most of the drinking places were beyond our pockets but there were some splendid air-conditioned cinemas which were reasonably priced and there was a very good servicemen's canteen which had been organised and set up by a delightful regal-looking lady of the Parsee faith who had cajoled, bossed and bullied the memsahibs from the various consulates as well as ladies from the churches and other women's fellowships, European, Indian, and Anglo-Indian, with some of their menfolk to work in the restaurant serving tables and sitting to talk with the servicemen — most of whom seemed to be British sailors. This was a treat which we had not experienced since we left home.

There was a small stage with a resident band and a microphone through which any young Bing Crosby sound-alike could offer his renditions.

Most interesting of all was imported British and Australian beer and stout, restricted to two large bottles per man per night, at the price of one rupee per bottle. A rupee was worth about one shilling and sixpence. We spent many a pleasant evening there. It was all that most of us could afford, and the good sahibs and mems tried their best not to be too patronising.

In the European section of Bombay there were quite a few schools of dancing which employed skilled ladies and gents, most of them of mixed race, to teach the ballroom exercises. This was a sport with which I was not very well acquainted, having apparently been born possessing two left feet.

The young Shetland lady who had beguiled my heart all that time ago was a very keen dancer and made it clear that in her opinion a man who could not dance was only half a man. I thought that here would be a good chance to learn the noble art so I went along with a few of the lads and enrolled with one of the schools where I really tried to learn how to navigate through the minefield of all this slow, slow, quick, quick, slow hellery. The other lads became quite good dancers but I was fully aware of my own capabilities. All that I desired was to be able to get safely around a dance floor without making too much of a fool of myself and I tried really hard to learn enough for that ambition. Eventually I could manage the waltz, foxtrot and quickstep as long as I had a partner who was accomplished, understanding and very patient. Friends said that I had mastered enough to get me by at a wedding or any similar function.

Years later, when I attended my own wedding dance it started with a Grand March and eightsome reel followed by Boston two-steps and all manner of other strange and terrible ritualistic movements clearly designed to mutilate the muscles of an uninitiated Englishman.

I still have two left feet.

One member of the ship's company who looked forward to a run ashore in Bombay was Jock the Dog. Jock was a mongrel with the head of a Labrador and the body of a Corgi. He had none of the bad temper of the Corgi but he was a friendly chap and most of us loved him. I am sure others far more intellectual than I must have already penned the saga of Jock — the dog with Chippendale legs.

He joined up with us in Haifa but he appeared to be neither a Jew nor an Arab. He attached himself to one particular group of seamen and always fell in with their part of the watch. He seemed to know every bugle call or pipe and obeyed them as far as they applied to him. He loved going ashore but he was quite content at sea.

During action stations he positioned himself in the sickbay flat and when the order came to 'Take cover' Jock knew exactly what it meant and he would dive under a locker and refuse to be pulled out by somebody who wanted the same hiding place. One day he found his way into the sickbay and dived under the very bed which the Medical Officer had reserved for his own shelter. I wonder if Jock fully understood the strange words of command he was given that day? Most of them probably began with the letters Ph.

I don't suppose he knew his father anyway.

Whenever we lay in harbour anywhere, Jock would wait on the quarterdeck sitting on his haunches until eight o'clock. I can see him yet — bringing himself to attention while 'Sticks' sounded Colours and the White Ensign was raised. He would then wait on the gangway for the eight-thirty duty boat on which he went across the harbour, and trot merrily on his way to carry out whatever activities sea dogs perform when they go ashore on leave or duty which, no doubt would include a dogfight or two. He always caught the eleven-thirty duty boat back to be in time for dinner.

When the seamen were sent to the army camp at Calabar, of course Jock had to go with his fellow duty men. He must have thought that this was a dog's paradise and he was reputed to have had his wicked way with half the lady dogs in Bombay — European only, of course.

East is east and west is west — even to a canny canine!

At the army camp there developed a bit of ill-feeling between the happy-go-lucky wartime sailors and the long-serving professional soldiers of the British Raj, probably because our inexperienced ratings were popular with the native bearers whom they were supposed to treat like lesser beings. One day, Jock the Dog was shot dead by an army sentry who claimed he thought it was a stray. Some believed him, thousands did not. Everybody in the camp knew Jock.

A few days later there was a prearranged boxing match between the army and the navy in which our team were easy victors. There followed a free-for-all among the khaki and blue spectators which ended with many of them being locked up for the night.

Poor old Jock the Dog would have loved that.

It seemed that somebody had got the message that the refit was going to take a lot longer than at first thought. A new stem had to be built from the keel up and each plate had to be riveted. The riveting was carried out by a gang of fierce looking Pathans from the North-west Frontier whose philosophy of life meant they should work only until they had earned sufficient cash to purchase weapons and then go back to the hills to carry on with their national sport of 'Shoot thy neighbour' until their cash flow problem forced them back to the dockyards. Naturally, those wise and blessed servants of the Great White Maharajah across the sea were not aware of this custom. It had only been going on for a few thousand years.

It began to look as if it was going to be a long two months.

Our holiday continued and half the ship's company at a time were sent up north to Deolali. This was an army transit camp and had been very much a forward base in the old days when there was regular fighting with the North-west Frontier tribes but it was now more of a leave centre. The name was pronounced 'Doolally'. You may have been there!

Here we had nothing to do except eat and sleep and be very well looked after by Indian native bearers who were far better educated than were most of us. Our particular attendant was a university student hoping to become a teacher. He was already a Master of Arts but required further qualifications before he could hope to progress far in a country where all the top jobs were reserved for sons of sahibs.

Our stay in Deolali was very pleasant and restful but we had to be constantly on guard against the Sikh chiropodists who would track down corns and ingrown toenails with the zeal of a hunter on safari after a man-eating tiger. There were also 'ear wallahs' who carried weird and wonderful appliances with which they would offer to remove the wax and any other harmless innocents which happened to like being there. We were warned to watch out for snakes. 'Sticks' told us that before he came to India he thought a puff adder was a man who farts in the bath and counts the bubbles.

It was not wise to report sick whatever your physical problem or you would be immediately whipped off to the local military hospital. One of our artificers asked for something to ease a slight problem of athlete's foot and found himself in an isolation ward wearing a red tie embroidered with a large 'V' sign which kept all the nurses and lady visitors well away from him. When some of the young lads spoke wistfully about being in hospital with all the lovely young nurses, 'Old Dave' would put a damper on it with the observation that, 'It takes away all the romance when she comes with the bedpan.' He said he once knew a hospital nurse who made herself a pair of panties out of a piece of surgical lint and it healed up!

One Sunday forenoon some of us visited the sergeants' mess where we quaffed the local beer, which was probably the most efficient laxative known to civilised man. An old reservist stoker petty officer — a very popular Geordie — was celebrating his birthday. He swallowed a bit too much of the brew and left the company rather hurriedly without saying goodbye. When we found him he had got as far as the door of the heads before he passed out and lay there, blissfully unaware in his nice clean white suit, looking for all the world as if somebody had scored a direct hit with a shovel full of you know what!

When he came to after we had helped to clean him up he said, 'My next trick, ladies and gentlemen, is impossible so I shall not attempt to do it!'

We had been languishing in Bombay for seven weeks when the supposedly friendly Japanese nation without as much as an 'excuse me' launched their treacherous attack on Pearl Harbour, followed by Hong Kong and most of the eastern territories of the British, French, Dutch and American empires which they very quickly overran against brave but hopelessly outnumbered opposition. In most of the fortified positions the guns were pointing the wrong way. Another example of halfwits in high places.

Anyway, the Americans were now fully involved in the conflict. Surely their great wealth and power would have to be the deciding factors even though they came in all behind like the cow's tail!

On the same day that we heard the news about Pearl Harbour, an American Coastguard navy transport ship carrying a party of Dutch soldiers on the way to Java arrived in Bombay. The American sailors knew nothing more about this significant event than we did, but, of course, they had come to win the war for us. Just like ourselves two years earlier, they were going to finish it all by Christmas. Poor devils, they had a lot to learn!

In fact they learned quite a bit a few nights later at a dance in the Town Hall when they decided to mix it with some of our boxing team as well as quite a few friendly Australians and lads from the Black Watch Regiment who were passing through Bombay at the time and felt that these men from the 'Yew Ess of A' should be taught a few of the facts of life.

This voluntary advanced education was prompted by an unprovoked attack on one of our favourite sportsmen — Joe, a good natured Londoner whom everybody liked. He joined the ship at Devonport as an able seaman after being called up with the first militia in 1939. In civvy street he earned his living as a professional heavyweight sparring partner. He was a clever, tough boxer but outside of the ring you would not find a more inoffensive fellow, a shy cuddly teddy bear of a man whose hobby was ballroom dancing at which he was very adroit for all his bulk, and this made him popular with the ladies.

That night a huge, six foot something American sailor took objection to Joe who was in the middle of the ballroom for the third time with a good looking girl whom our 'cousin' from across the Pond had been trying to chat up all evening.

He stopped Joe in his tracks towering over him aggressively.
'You don't like me, Limey, do ya?'
'Yes mate, I loves you, pleased to meet you.'
'Well I don't like you.'
He then threw a full-blooded punch to Joe's jaw which caused him to shake his head in bewilderment.

'Wot you do that for? I ain't done nuffink to you!'
'Put your hands up, ya yeller-bellied Limey bastard.'
'Nah, mate, no need to fall out, don't want no trouble.'
By this time the British and Australians were calling on Joe to show his capabilities.
'Come on Joe, let him have it.'
'Nah, nah, don't want no fuss, I'm here to dance.'
The man from Uncle Sam's navy obviously thought that Joe was scared of him.
'Stand up and fight, yer crawlin' Limey son-of-a-bitch before I kick your ass right back to where ya come from and all yer lousy English bums along with ya.'
Poor old Joe, there was nothing else for it, he had to give in. 'Sorry mate, nothing personal, no offence, honest.'
Whaam! — he hit the trouble-maker so hard that he slid right across the dance floor, landed among the wreckage of the plywood screen door, and lost all further interest in the proceedings.

The rest of the U.S. sailors started to mix it with Joe's mates and the soldiers — they should have known better. The one-sided argument was soon resolved and Joe carried on with the dance, apologising profusely to all the company including the American sailors who were still with us.

There's nothing like a good argument among friends!

The rapid advance of the Japanese forces through Burma had a marked effect on the idyllic life we had been enjoying in Bombay. India was now in the war seriously and was a prize which the ruthless little marauders were dearly anxious to capture, and there seemed to be no stopping them. In one naval action two of our battleships were battered to death by hordes of dive-bombers and torpedo carrying aircraft. Shortly after that another small British fleet was annihilated in the Java Sea. Singapore was easily and speedily overrun with many casualties and prisoners taken. Soon, refugees began flooding into Bombay.

The Japanese fleet was now at liberty to operate in the Indian Ocean so we had to start keeping R.D.F. watches and a constant lookout for saboteurs. We were warned to trust nobody at all.

We noticed that the pukka sahibs began to take more interest in the common servicemen, and invitations to private dinner parties and to some of the very restricted clubs began to pour in. The wealthy Indian aristocracy also chipped in with their two-penny worth and there were weekend trips to exotic places. Some of us who had been brought up during hard times could not help feeling uncomfortable with the thought that we were probably wasting as much food in one meal as the native Indian had to exist on for a week. We saw so much grinding poverty all around us, except in the European section.

There were many volumes to write about our stay in this part of the world and every man in the ship had his own story to tell although many would be better told by somebody else, or perhaps, more wisely left untold.

Like the four inebriated chief petty officers who were riding back to the dockyard in a horse drawn garry. They felt sorry for the horse so they got out and pulled the carriage themselves all the way to the ship where they paid the driver his full fare with a substantial tip before each of them kissed the stinking horse a maudlin farewell and wandered away in a veil of tears.

One chief petty officer who had been in Bombay five years earlier was impressed by the honesty and amazing memory of the owner of a Chinese laundry. In 1937, he had left two white drill suits there when his ship sailed earlier than expected. The day after we arrived he went back to the shop and as soon as he walked through the door the Chinaman spoke his name and produced a parcel containing two white suits with a laundry ticket from five years ago still attached.

In the hotel I shared a room with a regular service electrical artificer who was a very serious man but a bit of a card. One morning it was his birthday and he woke me up at the crack of dawn with a raucous shout of, 'Chads, Chads, look at this! Forty years old! Look at this!' proudly displaying his middle-age manhood. 'Look at this — forty years old.' He went next door to show his workmates. One of them was preparing to shave with an open razor and he made to strop it on the haughty appendage which immediately lost its enthusiasm.

Our young Paymaster Lieutenant was married in Bombay to a lovely lady who was the daughter of the Swedish Consul and he invited all the staff to the wedding. The celebration consisted of an afternoon of pompous praises and paraphrases but the champagne was good.

We had a romantic young ship's cook named 'Slinger' who fell in love with a rich Indian native lady and ran away with her. We never heard of them again.

I think that what made the most lasting impression on me was the professional skill of the Indian artisans. I saw carpenters using small ancient tools to saw, drill, carve, shape, smooth, and polish pieces of rough timber which they held using their feet for a vice, to produce superb furniture.

I watched a gang of men erecting a tall, handsome building laying huge blocks of precision-cut stone using no more sophisticated lifting equipment than a set of sheerlegs powered by a host of labourers hauling on a long rope.

I gazed open-mouthed at a party of unconcerned coolies stepping gaily heel to heel and toe to toe carrying between them a grand piano inverted and balanced on their heads. All it needed was a musical accompaniment.

We did not see much of the Indian ladies except for the poor downtrodden creatures going about doing all the very lowly paid menial tasks like scrubbing and cleaning. At that time, even in the big cities, the Indian woman was very much the property of her father or husband and had no rights of her own. She was betrothed very early in life, often at birth — almost 'made to order' in a business arrangement between her father and his associates, just as it had been in the civilised west not all that long ago. When she was only nine or ten years old she became a bride, maybe to a man three times her age. It was sad to think of a little girl becoming a mother and often a slave for her in-laws at the age when kids back home were still playing with their dolls. That was the way of life in eastern culture; no doubt things will be much better in modern times.

We met a few European women but they were mostly army nurses or daughters of the white Raj, but they were strictly officer material. The majority of the girls who worked in shops and offices were of mixed race whom we knew as Anglo-Indians. They were good-looking, friendly ladies but their main hope in life was to marry a white man and go with him to live in Europe where they fondly believed that there would be no such thing as racial discrimination. To this end they kept themselves chaste since any woman known to have a man was looked upon as a prostitute. So, alas, the poor young sailor laddie could only dream.

There was a story about a nosey English lady on board a passenger ship in Bombay who leaned too far over the guard rail and fell head first into the rubbish lighter which had just come alongside. The Indian refuse collector was heard to remark, 'English sahib very wasteful. This one good for at least five more years!'

Like most sailors our ship's company managed to get along with the local people wherever we were and in Bombay they seemed to be popular with the native Indians as well as the Europeans and those of mixed race. By merely showing the 'wogs' a bit of respect — which was strange to them — we received wonderful co-operation from the dockyard civil servants and craftsmen — far more than we ever received in Devonport or Portsmouth.

Of course, all the senior civil servants had to be British. They were pen-pushers from home who had been made R.N.V.R. Lieutenants attached to the Royal Indian Navy and set above their far more learned counterparts in Bombay. We ignored them! It was far more pleasant working with the local people.

At the start of the New Year the riveters came back from the hills and it seemed that they were going to finish the job at last, so we started getting the ship together again,

We had the pleasure of a new Captain — our fourth since 1939 — and there were a few new officers but most of the warrant officers and chief petty officers were still with us. The 'Old Fireater' had left us for his own command and his next in line was given a half-stripe and took his place as First Lieutenant.

The new Skipper had been a survivor from one of the battleships recently sunk by the Japanese navy and that did not sound too promising.

Before we settled back aboard, the ship had to be fumigated using the newly-discovered D.D.T. to get rid of the cockroaches which seemed to bother those in authority more than they bothered us. We thought they were friendly little things. When you opened your locker door, scores of them would come rushing out to meet you and one mess mate swore that he had trained them to sort out whatever garment he wanted to wear at the time and bring it out to him. We used to hold races with them along the mess table and many a bob or two changed hands over the winner.

The old sailors warned us it was very unwise to get rid of the cockroaches, and how right they were. A few weeks later the ship was lousy with bedbugs and we never did get rid of those horrible creatures.

We did not manage to get rid of the rats either, which seemed to have joined us at the same time and place. It was 'love's labour lost' as the monkey said when he fondled a bag of tacks — or words to that effect.

1942 saw a change of life for the Jack Dusty and his faithful fountain pen on ships of this class and others on canteen messing when those illustrious lights of the great establishment, in their never-faltering zeal for imposing unwanted alteration, decided that this system of feeding the brutes just would not do. Nobody asked the opinion of the workers, but then, they never did.

Until now, every man had been given a small but reasonably adequate 'standard ration' of meat, vegetables, flour, fats, tea, sugar, and milk plus a small monetary payment with which to purchase other edible extravagances from the ship's provisions or the N.A.A.F.I. canteen. If the cash allowance was not fully taken up the balance was paid back to each mess after deduction of any sums due for replacement of lost mess traps, particularly cutlery which was liable to be poured down the gash chute with the dishwater causing the mess cooks to recite, 'Tinkle, tinkle little spoon, a knife and fork will follow soon.' The supply staff had to produce an elaborate statement of these lurid details which was pinned to the mess deck notice board at the end of every month.

It was considered by those up there that some of the men were picking up too much mess savings and must therefore be starving themselves for the sake of a few extra coppers in their money belts. In their great wisdom the powers that be decided to abolish the standard ration and instead give the men an extra shilling or three in victualling allowance with which to purchase their food as they so wished. The leading hand of the mess was in charge of the catering and each one had his own ideas.

One leading stoker, fed up with his messmates grumbling, purchased a lot of tinned food from the pusser's store including small tins of corned beef and generally disliked oval shaped tins of herring, usually referred to as 'herrings in'. The stokers set all the tins up in the mess shelves to resemble 1918 army tanks. The monthly statement showed that this mess had well overspent its allowance and the Captain commended the leading hand for looking after his men's well-being.

A dedicated leading seaman known as 'Honest John' purchased very little from the ship's stores but spent most of his mates' allowance on more appetizing fresh food purchased ashore, often chipping in an extra bob or two of his own. His men were better fed than most of us, but of course the monthly statement showed the mess account to be in credit and poor old John received a right royal rollicking for his efforts.

Meanwhile I had been moved back to Central Stores and was once more a 'deep sea ironmonger'. I was never keen on this job, especially at sea. The main store was below deck and it meant that I must race up to the bridge every time I had to open and close the watertight hatch. I was also expected to be able to identify whatever tool or appliance anybody wanted, even if the man himself did not know what he was talking about. Once a mechanic came to the store, waved his finger in a spiral motion and demanded, 'Something that goes up into'.

Ah well, I always wanted to be a sailor — serves me glad!

A few months later I was shifted again, this time to Clothing and Mess Traps which was less demanding, except that it meant handling a fair amount of cash. I had to see to the supply and sale of uniform clothing to officers and men, which duty like everything else in this establishment demanded a great deal of form filling and precise bookkeeping. I was also responsible for tobacco and toilet paper.

I now had experience as a petty officer in three departments of the supply rating's duty and I was only twenty-three years of age but I still had a great deal to learn. Being a petty officer was not much more glamorous than a supply assistant, but at least the uniform looked a bit less like that of a bus conductor.

It was April by the time a rejuvenated *Coventry* closed the Gateway of India behind her and we started to make our way back to our old stamping ground.

It was a strange, rather exhilarating sensation. We had been ashore for so long that our feet were starting to grow 'earth-bound'. In the four-and-a-half years since I joined the Royal Navy I had always lived and worked on a moving ship which had seemed a natural home to me until we were forced into this alien shore life — and a lazy pointless life at that. I was getting used to it and did not want to wake up.

But as soon as I felt the heave of the old deck and the cool wind in my face I suddenly felt whole again. Life always seemed so much cleaner at sea.

Going over the water to Aden we spent a few days doing sea trials, getting used to a ship with a well patched-up hull and a brand new bow, all nice and newly painted, inside and out. And there were exciting new toys to play with in the shape of Oerlikon guns. These weapons fired one pound shells accurately and rapidly with a far greater range than the useless old point-fives and could be very handy against dive-bombers. They were a foreign invention of course which had been tried out on this ship in 1938, appreciated by the gunners who used them, but rejected by those with the broad stripes and balls and things. They could have saved many a life in Narvik and Crete.

From now on we had to keep a tight defence watch since we were within range of the Japanese navy. We were not fitted with underwater detection equipment so we depended on our lookouts to ensure that we were not surprised by an adventurous Nippon submarine commander.

We spent a few hours in Aden then steamed on into the stifling heat of the Red Sea which certainly helped to take off some of the extra pounds of fat we had gained during our sumptuous living in Bombay. Our only travelling companions were hundreds of playful little flying fishes some of which landed on our deck where the poor things expired.

On our way to Suez we were met by an imposing looking Arab dhow which drew up alongside with some 'diplomatic message'. After plenty of bowing and scraping which did tend to give one's rear end a nippy taste we carried on with our journey while the Saudi craft sailed off into the sunset — not a very easy task to accomplish as he happened to be heading east at the time. *We don't get much money but we do see life!*

At Port Taufiq we noticed a lot of changes since we had been there six months previously. For one thing there were quite a few W.R.N.S. stationed here now — talkative ones at that, who seemed to know far more than we did about our goings and doings. The complete lack of security was not very encouraging. Later on we were to wonder if this was accident or design.

After two nights in Port Taufiq we passed through the still familiar Suez Canal and tied up in Port Said. There was not much change here, except a few more wrecks, and we could still almost recognise every grain of sand on the banks. Next day we headed for Alexandria where we tied up at our old berth on Kamari Mole. This time we had to have an anti-torpedo lighter moored alongside us, which was something we had not heard about before. We had always felt reasonably safe out here.

Many things had happened while we were indulging ourselves in the mystic east and now that we were back to the war we began to feel like skivers. There was little left of the once powerful Eastern Mediterranean Fleet. Most of the heavy and light cruisers had been sunk or badly damaged with great loss of life. Force K from Malta had been destroyed by mines while here two battleships including the flagship along with a destroyer and a fleet tanker had been crippled in one attack by Italian frogmen with limpet mines despite regular depth-charging of the Grand Harbour. This brilliant operation could only have been achieved with help from ashore, but the trouble was that we did not really know just who were our enemies. There were spies everywhere. As one chap put it, 'Nearly as many agents as arseholes.'

The Desert Army had broken its bonds, raised the siege of Tobruk and advanced as far west as Benghazi only to be forced right back to El Alamein where they were needing all the help they could get to hold out.

The Commander-in-Chief Admiral Cunningham had been recalled to London and replaced by a less experienced Admiral who had no fleet anyway. There seemed to be a feeling of weariness among the sailors who had been doing our share of the work lately, including our sister ship *H.M.S. Carlisle*.

We had expected too much when first Russia and then America had been forced into the war. At the moment they seemed to be in a worse state than we were. But that would surely change once they got their acts together. In the meantime we just had to carry on rewardless. At least we ourselves had enjoyed a long break, so we ought to be in good shape and raring to go; pity nobody would tell us where we were going — not that it would make any difference.

Despite the beliefs of their Lordships and the equally humourless propaganda merchants there was not really despondency among those on the mess deck. However grim might things be there were plenty of natural comics to lighten the day with a rude remark and most of those of working class origin had a love of laughter; it was in their nature.

If a sailor was fed up he would usually say he was 'chocka' and the wise and wonderful upkeepers of the fleet's morale decided that this word was one of the seven deadly sins and its use must be forbidden on pain of castigation or something sounding similar. Of course the lads used all kinds of adjectives to take its place, much to the confusion of those in authority.

None of us thought about actually losing the war. We were British — or English or Scottish or Welsh or Irish — we always won our wars even if we lost a few battles on the way. Anyway, our sense of humour got us further than all the fighting skills in the world. But it was getting to be hard going after nearly three years of it. 'Old Vic' believed that it made no difference anyway. 'When we've won the war the politicians and civil servants will only make a **ck-up of the peace like they did the last time.'

My office was on the stokers' mess deck where I had a lot of friends and one night a chap pushed open the door saying, ‘Come and see this for a laugh’, and what a laugh it was.

I saw four stokers all stark naked except for colourful neckties, worn by each of them, which they had salvaged from a bag of cleaning rags. They held a wooden handspike up to their lips like a gigantic four-man flute as they bobbed up and down with their unmentionables swinging full and free in rhythm with the ragtime music coming from the wireless, to which they were keeping good time, with all the mess deck cheering them on. Probably the Holy Joes would have been aghast at such lewd and libidinous behaviour but I did not see much despondency there!

Of course, the greatest morale booster we could have was a letter from home and, despite all the hazards and difficulties, we still received a steady flow of mail. Many of the messages from our friends and relatives did **not** get through and the lucky ones were about six weeks old by the time they caught up with us but they were eagerly awaited and could mean such a lot.

When the postman called out our names it was rather sad to see the faces of those for whom there was nothing. Some poor chaps seemed to be all alone in the world and often a messmate would ask a sister or a friend to write to one of those lads. It fairly cheered him up.

Generally it was the ladies, bless them, who did the writing. Letters came from mothers, wives, sisters, girlfriends, or even strangers who thought that some lonely serviceman in a far-flung outpost of the British Empire might appreciate a pen-pal or two.

Some long-lasting correspondence, even romance, came through the lads finding addresses which working girls had slipped into packing crates and cartons. I remember finding a wee note among a pair of Barr and Stroud binoculars and I gave it to a Glasgow rating who said that he would write to the lady but he left the ship a few weeks later and I did not hear if anything developed. I often wondered. It could have made a lovely story.

I used to look forward to receiving a letter from the Shetland lady with whom I had fallen in love in the long distant past. Was it really only two years ago? Lilian had joined the Women’s Land Army and was at the time working like a slave for a greedy old Scottish farmer in the primitive conditions of an old Aberdeenshire steading. Despite this back-breaking job she always found something interesting and cheerful to tell me. Her mother also wrote to me now and then and they both exchanged notes with my mother although they had never met.

People derived a lot of comfort from sending and receiving letters and most folks were able to write and read. Friendly competitions like spelling-bees and general knowledge quizzes were popular among all walks of life, especially in pubs or clubs and factory canteens.

For the most part, the news that we received from home was bright and cheery and it said very little about the hardship and adversity that our loved ones had to endure, but we all knew very well that everything in the garden was not exactly a blaze of sunshine.

Food rations were just enough to keep body and soul together with nothing to spare and there were very few luxuries. At the time that servicemen out here were able to enjoy a substantial ration of meat and fats and all the lovely fresh fruit we could eat of the kind they never saw, the womenfolk back home spent hour after hour standing in queues looking for any little extra which they hoped might be for sale at not more than twice its normal price. Yet even those long waiting lines became a venue for cheery and friendly gossip.

Life could be very drab, especially for those who had to herd their young children into air raid shelters every night. Indiscriminate bombing continued relentlessly and there were many civilian casualties but the British women were a sturdy race and mothers and wives kept most of their anxiety and despair to themselves. They did not wish to burden their menfolk with all their troubles when they were fighting so far away from home. In fact sometimes these same ladies saw more fighting than we did.

Naturally, home news was not always good tidings for everybody. One shipmate had word of the death of his parents and then most of his kinfolk in different air raids. At first he was angry, then bitter, but by the time the fourth report came to him he was past caring. Another chap heard that his fiancée had been gunned down by a playful German airman as she strolled innocently along by the beach near her home. From then on, his only desire was to see lots of dive-bombers through the sites of his Oerlikon machine-gun.

Most of my friends from school days had joined up at the start of the war and many of them were killed or captured. Sometimes I would receive a letter from a mother telling me of her son's fate. Some of the letters I had to answer could be very sad.

Damn the Hun, and the Wop, and the Nip and all their snivelling friends.

Most of us enjoyed writing home but it was not easy to express our feelings when we knew that our letters were going to be pored over and censored by some young officer and perhaps joked about in the wardroom. There was not a great deal about which we could write, anyway. We were not allowed to harbour private thoughts and keeping a personal diary was a criminal offence — if you were caught.

Officers who censored our correspondence would cut out any word they did not like so we had to avoid writing on both sides of the page. Some of the lads would include in their letters suggestive remarks as a way of hinting at their private opinion of a superior, for the benefit of the officer who would have to peruse their writing. Such remarks might be: 'Hope the censor enjoys this — if he can read long hand.' 'Wonder if he's married?' 'Wonder if his father and mother are married?' 'Do prostitutes ever get married? — course they do. Where do you think sub-lieutenants come from?'

A few years ago I came across a letter written by a Shetland sailor to his grandmother in 1941. The first sentence was, 'The Captain of this ship is a pure Count and so are all the officers!' For some reason that article of enlightenment had been left alone while nearly every other word had been snipped out so that the whole page looked like a bit of lace. It would have been bewildering to the old lady but it was a work of art by the censor.

Some of the younger ratings were glad to talk about their news from loved ones despite being teased by their older messmates. One lad from the wilds of Devon used to boast about his three months old son who was making good progress — very good for a child who was born more than a year after we left England. He was not very good at arithmetic either. An older man advised him to watch out for enemies back home as it was obvious that one of them had it in for him. Another fellow thought that his baby was deformed when his wife wrote that he had grown another foot!

There was always plenty of fatherly advice from the old-timers, such as, 'A woman should be kept like a racehorse, well shod and well ridden' or 'The ideal wife would be a deaf and dumb nymphomaniac who keeps a pub'. 'Old Bungy' said he hoped he would be going home soon because his wife who was in the Wrens had just been made a petty officer and he wanted to fulfil a life's ambition.

I was lucky never to be short of a letter because I was one of a large family. We all took some part in the war and between us we saw quite a bit of action although nothing spectacular.

Father, being on the wrong side of sixty, was too old for the army so he joined the War Department Police Service and whiled away the nights keeping armed guard over military establishments such as ammunition dumps. Mother spent a lot of time with the Women's Voluntary Service (W.V.S.) and other such organisations, also doing a stint as a fire-watch lookout on the roof of a tall building.

Oldest brother Tom was with the Royal Artillery operating searchlights on the south-east coast where the bombers came over nearly every night. Brothers Jack and Geoffrey were stokers in the Royal Navy while sister Grace had already served two years in the Wrens (Women's Royal Naval Service). Later during the war she became the wife of a submariner in the Royal Netherlands Navy.

So far, Jack had seen more excitement than the rest of us. He had started the war in fleet destroyer *H.M.S. Jaguar*, taking part in the fighting at Narvik and Dunkirk, then the battles in the Mediterranean before transferring to the sloop *H.M.S. Auckland* to take part in the evacuation of Greece and Crete, and the 'Tobruk Ferry'. He survived the sinking of *Auckland* at Tobruk and was now serving on *H.M.S. Resource*.

Youngest brother David was a very enthusiastic fifteen year old would-be soldier with the Local Defence Volunteers and enlisted in the Royal Marines as soon as he was old enough.

Sister Saidie, not yet eighteen, was with the Voluntary Ambulance Service and older sisters Linda and Beryl were working on farms. Oldest sister Cissie stayed in Portsmouth helping with the A.R.P. and keeping a home for her sailor husband Alfred, who was serving on the aircraft carrier *H.M.S. Illustrious* at the time.

A local newspaper thought it worthwhile writing an article about the family's war effort and Dad said it was only right to let the history writers know that there **were** a few English folk helping with the fighting. Surely we were tarred with a large measure of very good luck because the whole family came through the conflict with all our bits and pieces still attached. But it would have been a lot of worry for our mother, like all mothers, in those heart-weary years.

We remained in Alexandria for the next three or four weeks, steaming a few miles out of harbour for exercises each day. We fairly missed our former First Lieutenant. 'Old Rumple' had a way of putting a bit of fun into training unlike our present Number One, known as the 'Cargo Buster' who had been with us since the war began and was said never to smile unless it was absolutely necessary to carry out an order. He had been trained to work with Lascars, and it showed.

It was a pity really, because he had been a good officer and very fair. When I was on a previous ship with him he taught me to swim.

At the start of June we prepared for another of those travels to places of mystery. We took on a load of 'secret' mail with addresses in Malta and then we left for our next destination which happened to be Port Said. Here we joined up with a few Hunt class destroyers escorting some merchant ships and headed west.

This was the first real test for our new bows, new Captain, new armament, new officers, and many new ratings — some neurotics. Fortunately there was still enough of the old crowd left to show them the ropes.

We steamed west, then north. Only the Captain had any idea where we were going — at least we hoped he had. We assumed that our destination would be Malta and that would certainly be no 'Happy Hour'. We were shadowed all the way by enemy long-range aircraft and we had a visit from some Royal Air Force Beaufighters who shot down a shadower which came too close, and were lucky not to be shot down themselves by inexperienced gunners on another cruiser who mistook them for J.U. 88's.

Suddenly we turned back east and we thought that the venture had been called off. We harboured further doubts just before sunset when we fought off a mass attack by Stukas and J.U.88s.

We were back in business!

Before we left Alexandria we had acquired two strange additions to the wardroom, which we assumed were something to do with something. One of the peculiar party was a Royal Air Force Officer whose speciality appeared to have something to do with Fighter Direction. We hoped he could direct a few fighters our way — if he could find any.

The other chap was a War Correspondent — first time we had qualified for one of these. When he saw our pom-pom in action he was heard to remark, 'Surely nothing can get through a barrage like that'. Actually nothing ever did get past 'Buck' and his Chicago Piano. The trouble was that it was in the fore part of the ship while most of the dive-bombing attacks came from behind — the Dirty Boche!

During the first day's attack, one of the merchant ships was damaged and ordered to make for Tobruk while another freighter could not maintain speed and was sent back to Alexandria. There followed a quiet night with occasional bursts of star shell on the horizon which showed that the enemy was still looking for us, or for some other body.

The next afternoon we met and joined up with a fairly large convoy protected by Rear Admiral Vian and his light cruiser squadron with a number of destroyers, corvettes and minesweepers. We never liked being in somebody else's convoy. We always seemed to have more success when we took charge ourselves. We were probably there only as a lure for the Italian fleet anyway.

We were so often used as bait that we began to feel like a can of worms or some such object. But at least we had been in action again and found out that we could still give a good account of ourselves.

Later on we learned that this had been a desperate attempt to supply beleaguered Malta with convoys from both east and west in the hope and belief that at least a few ships would get through, but nobody told us this at the time.

The popular radio show 'ITMA' with Tommy Handley had a catchphrase, 'They don't tell nobody nuffink, nowadays.' And how right they were!

Among the warships in Rear Admiral Vian's forces was the ancient battle-cruiser *H.M.S. Centurion*. Long before the war she had been demilitarised and used as a fleet target ship, controlled by radio. She had recently been built up and camouflaged to impersonate the new battleship *H.M.S. King George V* with 'bridge', 'fighting' top and fifteen-inch 'gun turrets' made out of plywood, and large wooden tubes to represent the huge guns.

Unfortunately, while under repair in Capetown a few weeks previously, somebody had spotted two young sailors cheerfully carrying one of these 'gun barrels' between them and doubts had been cast on their authenticity.

This did not fool the high-level bomber crews but it did surprise those who came in close to find that she was bristling with real short-range weapons. She shot down quite a few dive-bombers during one day's action while she endured a number of direct hits and near misses to her old hulk that would have sunk half a dozen modern ships. We heard through our usual grapevine that she was carrying grain for Malta and was then to be sent out under radio control to scuttle and block the entrance to one of the enemy-held North African harbours.

Our plot to entice the Italian fleet for a surprise attack did not tempt anybody. The Italian Admiral preferred to wait with his battle wagons until his own chosen time when he believed that he would be able to bring all his big guns against us in one glorious shebang.

In the darkest hour before the dawn we were approaching the part of our journey where we were in most danger — one of the 'Bomb Alleys' where we were in range of attack from both Cyrenaica and Crete but too far away for help from our own air force if we had any fighters left.

Enemy aircraft attacks started in the early afternoon and pressed on until dark. We were in the middle of the convoy and were in action for five hours with hardly time to draw breath — or expel it. There were screaming Stukas and torpedo-bombers everywhere. It was noisy, to say the least.

One of our particular charges was a petrol tanker. We had to make sure that she was not hit or we should all have gone out together, and we were only just good friends.

Then the Commander-in-Chief back in Cleopatra's country came up with the great idea that the convoy should change direction again and make the Wops believe that we were throwing our hand in and going home.

We had to go through the fearful manoeuvre of turning the convoy about while under continuous air attack and completely illuminated by enemy flares.

The German torpedo-boat commander at Crete must have thought that Christmas had come early this year. He probably never had a chance like that during his whole career. Attacks by E-boats and torpedo-bombers carried on all through the night and the next day.

We moved to the outer fringe of the convoy, putting us between the merchant ships and the attacks coming from Crete. Our guns were red hot and the empty brass shell cases, all of which had to be salvaged, were becoming a menace. We had neither the time to collect them nor the place to store them until the action ceased for the length of time they needed to cool down. In due course, the books would have to show so many shells used, so many empties returned. People were fussy about figures.

All day long the attacks continued as if the enemy had a limitless supply. Although he now had a Russian front to contend with Hitler seemed to have more bombers for the Mediterranean than ever before. Where the hell were they all coming from?

We moved back into the middle of the convoy with our 'friend' the petrol tanker tucked in close by. We had not much idea of what was happening to the rest of the ships but thus far we had kept all our own charges safe. However the escort force had already lost five destroyers, while two heavy cruisers had been severely damaged.

A few days earlier the cruiser *H.M.S. Newcastle* had steamed past us into Alexandria harbour with her Royal Marine Band blowing their hearts out with her signature tune 'Blaydon Races'. The next morning she had led us out in the same blaze of glory calling for ironic cheers from our own Royal Marines manning their obsolete guns on their old-fashioned quarterdeck. During the night she had become one of the victims of the E-boat attacks but had managed to patch-up the damage and carry on.

The next forenoon while changing escort positions during a lull in the action she limped along close by us with her damaged bows showing their wounds — causing a great cheer from our bootnecks and the cry, 'Where's your f*****g band now?' It was only fun, of course.

We learned later that while we carried on our yo-yo action of advancing and retreating another convoy was continuing to push towards Malta from the west and suffering very heavy losses. Eventually only two of the western convoy's merchant ships made it into Malta. Their cargo was sufficient to keep the islanders heads up for a bit longer, but they were finding it very hard going, very hard indeed.

Still plodding on with a progress which seemed to us like one pace forward and two paces back, our force lost another cruiser and two more destroyers and all of us were now practically out of ammunition and low on fuel. There was nothing for it but to fight our way back to Alexandria with what we had left.

We finally reached our berth at C.2 mole with our magazines empty and our fuel tanks almost dry. Somebody told us we had been with operation 'Vigorous'.

It had been a failure — but it was certainly vigorous!

We spent the next three days in harbour cleaning away the grime of last week's battle, replenishing stores, fuel and ammunition and sending a few men ashore to cells for being bad boys. It was a wonder we were not all locked up by now.

The Commander-in-Chief paid us a visit to tell us the good news that the war was not going very well. The Desert Army was in full retreat from some German upstart general by the name of Rommel. But we were going to hold onto Tobruk at all costs. Which is why we were not at all surprised the next day when we heard that the desert fortress had fallen.

Expecting the worst, the Admiral decided to disperse what was left of the fleet to bases in Beirut, Haifa and Port Said. A small liner packed with Women's Royal Naval personnel was sent to Port Taufiq where the ship became a staff office. We were sent through the Suez Canal and then down to transit anchorage at 'Abu Cadabra' or something like that to act as anti-aircraft guard. Enemy airfields were now only a hundred and sixty miles away from Alexandria and Suez.

We spent most of July escorting ships up and down the Gulf of Suez without seeing much action. We did one trip through the canal to Port Said where we spent a week drafting home some more of our experienced crew and replacing them with officers and men straight out of training. Some of them were so green that they thought the **foretop** was something to do with genital surgery on the children of Israel.

I was surprised to learn that some otherwise quite intelligent chaps were really illiterate and I tried to help by encouraging them to try and read one of the books in our very modest 'library'. I came across one fellow absorbed in an Oxford Dictionary and asked him what he thought of it. His reply was quite enlightening, 'Not much of a story but the writer fairly explains himself!'

It was not particularly encouraging but what did it matter? Surely we would all be going home soon one way or another. At the beginning of August we were through the Suez again and spent two nights in Beirut. From there we went to Haifa to make ready for what we thought was another Malta convoy.

We left Haifa and joined up with a squadron of light cruisers, a flotilla of destroyers, and some merchant ships heading west. We stooged around for a few days without meeting any attacks we could not deal with then we were ordered back to Beirut. Afterwards we learned that we had again been used as a decoy to split the enemy forces while 'Operation Pedestal' fought its way through to Malta. Of course our strategy fooled nobody except us. The 'Pedestal' convoy managed to get only four ships through to Malta at great loss of shipping and lives. Among the escorts lost was our sister ship *H.M.S. Cairo*, one of the original six converted 'C' class cruisers. There were only half of us left now.

One of the ships that did fight her way through was the vital tanker *Ohio* which probably meant the survival of the island. Every man on that ship ought to have been awarded the Victoria Cross. But she was not a warship was she?

After a few days in Beirut it was back through the Canal to Port Taufiq and then to the anchorage down in the Gulf. From there we became very busy escorting a steady flow of ships between the Horn of Africa and Suez, including the huge liners *Queen Mary*, *Queen Elizabeth* and *Mauretania* carrying between them many thousands of British troops for the Eighth Army which had recently been taken over by Generals Alexander and Montgomery.

It was quite a humbling experience seeing these great ships — two of them the biggest vessels in the world, all British built and the proudest liners afloat. We seemed so insignificant in their presence, especially when they had to reduce speed so we could escort them. They were far better armed than we were, having been fitted out in America with all the most up-to-date weapons and accoutrements. They were certainly a great help to the war effort. With their speed and carrying capability they could shift a whole army in a few days.

Surely with all the reinforcement of men and material we saw pouring into Suez there must be something big going to happen but it was unlikely that anybody would tell us about it. 'Not good to let the chaps know too much, old fellow, gives them ideas, don't you know!' 'Top secret, and all that, what?' Ah well, we could always ask the Arabs!

Meantime, for the remainder of August we spent our time sweating up and down the Red Sea escorting heavily laden ships to Suez and taking back the empties as fast as they could turn around. Much to our surprise we saw very little interference by enemy aircraft. In fact we began to see Royal Air Force fighters now and then. Not often enough to get used to them, but it was nice to know that they were there. We hoped that they would call along again sometime.

One day we had to visit the British Protectorate Zanzibar — setting for many a stirring novel and film, probably written by authors who had never seen the place. The bulk of shipping in the small, sleepy port seemed to be Arab dhows but here and there the White Ensign of a sloop or gunboat tried to make its presence known. We were told that Zanzibar was a very busy place before the war and the harbour used to be filled with merchants from every corner of the globe. We were not given much time ashore but managed to look around the nearby habitat.

The narrow main street was a long avenue of bazaars trading in jewellery and various local crafts as well as silks, cottons and spices — sacks and sacks of spices, particularly their home grown cloves which filled the air with a not unpleasant aroma, doing its best to camouflage other less enchanting smells. The stall holders were dark-skinned Arabs dressed in colourful, long flowing robes and wearing huge turbans. The scene could have come straight out of 'Arabian Nights'. We did not see 'Ali-Baba' but we met a few of his forty thieves!

Such women as put in an appearance — at least we imagined that they were of the fair sex — were draped from head to heel in black, shapeless gowns and hoods with only a small aperture in front of their faces so that they could know where they were going. We did not get close enough to tell the colour of their eyes as they were under the protection of fierce looking black-skinned eunuchs and we did not wish to tangle with these men who had nothing to lose.

The blast from the ship's siren reminded us that our shore leave was over and it was time to say 'farewell to this romantic island'. We had not managed to visit any of the notorious slave auctions, nor did we catch sight of Dorothy Lamour.

On 3rd September 1942, three years to the day after war broke out, we passed through the Suez Canal for our twelfth time and tied up in Port Said. There was a change from the last time we were there which was only about a month ago. There seemed to be very few men around and the Staff Office and Supply Offices were apparently in the no doubt capable hands of the ladies of the Wrens. And what a 'speak-easy' that was. There was more chatter than a crows' court, and the ladies seemed to know everything about everything and everybody.

We, of course, were completely ignorant as to our next move. Our Captain could not even say what time it was without opening sealed orders and even then he would probably tell us only where the big hand of the clock pointed. Everybody else in Egypt seemed to know where we were going to and what for, but we never paid attention to buzzes even though they often turned out to be true.

The 'Jim Irish' boys told us that we were bound for Tobruk and just in case we did not get back alive could they have their dhobi money and anything else we owed them now, please. The lady Wrens seemed to have the same idea about our destination and told us to take care.

So we were going to Tobruk? What of it, we had been there before and should probably have to go there again. It had never been a trip that folks queued up to take, and the harbour was full of wrecks but it was all part of a sailor's life. We had not been told officially and we did not believe it anyway, but it would do for a conversation starter. The weather was never anything to talk about out here.

We spent the next few days filling up with fuel and ammunition as well as a sufficient quantity of stores and provisions to make it look as if we were going on a long voyage. Perhaps we were but we hoped not because our winter woollies had not yet arrived.

There were further changes in the ship's company with many of the old hands drafted home or elsewhere including Charlie, the chief pusser, which left me as the senior rating of the accountant division except for 'Old Vic', the chef. Our complement of supply ratings had been halved in recent weeks. All my mates had left — some without replacement. First to go was 'Spud', then Pete, two chums who had been with me on the ship when the war started. Then went 'Witty', 'Sheila' and 'Wash-deck-locker Wilf' — three young lads who had joined us as 'sprogs' a few months later. We had trained them up to become petty officers and as such they were needed elsewhere. Led by Charlie who taught us most of what we knew we had been a 'family' for nearly three years and that was a long commission in wartime.

Together we had served under four captains and four paymaster commanders. Now Charlie had been drafted and I was left 'in charge'. Suddenly, I felt rather lonely. Senior officers and ratings were replaced by youngsters who were given temporary higher status. My new boss was a lieutenant promoted to acting lieutenant commander taking on the accountant officer's duties. He was a very fine chap, too. It seemed as if they were getting rid of everybody except the 'expendable' — like disposing of all the valuables before burning down the house for its insurance. I suppose I was included in the gash!

There was a message there but we did not notice it at the time. We had got past the stage of even thinking about it. Fortunately, the older Warrant Officers were still with us and, my goodness, we were thankful for that.

The Warrant Officers, later titled 'Commissioned Warrant Officers' were really the backbone of the Royal Navy. Most of them had served their time from boy rating to chief petty officer before being commissioned. They lived in their own mess quarters and were still not classed as wardroom material so they were a buffer between the upper and lower deck. They knew just about everything there was to know about the navy in general and their own branch in particular and everybody trusted them. We needed them now more than ever because some of us, although we would not care to voice the subject, had been convinced for a while that our new Captain and long-suffering First Lieutenant were 'away with the fairies'.

So we gathered all the rumours together and decided that Malta was probably the best bet. Then we had our meal, wrote a letter or two and carried on as usual, just the same old routine. We were under sailing orders so there was no shore leave. The condemned men ate a hearty supper and to blazes with the mess savings.

We slipped and steamed out at midnight very secretly under sealed orders which the Captain would open at the appropriate time and place. He would then tell us what it was all about if he thought that we needed to know.

We learned later that just about everybody in Egypt (and Germany) knew that we were going to accompany a landing party to capture Tobruk, destroy its defences and leave again before they knew what hit them. We had heard it before but it was too daft to believe.

Meeting with two Tribal class destroyers carrying small landing craft slung from their davits made some people think things, especially the old hands. A flotilla of larger-sized landing craft escorted by motor torpedo-boats straggled along hugging the North African coast as closely as they dared.

Apparently the M.T.B.s were to create a diversion by attacking shipping and defence positions inside the harbour while the destroyers and other ships would land five hundred Royal Marines who were to join forces with about half that number of men from the Long Range Desert Group and surround the German forces.

I was thinking of the Irish song 'Slattery's Mounted Fut.'

To them upstairs it would probably seem a routine job. They sent less than a thousand riflemen to capture and destroy a very sound fortification defended by many times their number of highly trained and well-armed German soldiers who already knew when and where they were going to land.

'Simple job — don't bother me with numbers and details, old boy. Just send in the Marines and all that sort of thing, knock 'em for six, tally ho, good show. 'Nother G. and T. old chap?'

In the wash place that night I was speaking to a bomb-happy stoker petty officer who told me he had survived the sinking of five ships during the last year. Each time he had been kitted out with the bare necessities and given £10 to purchase the rest of his kit. He told us cheerfully that he had never bothered to buy any new gear but had a great time spending the money. He was obviously a Jonah and I'm sure if we had known this beforehand he would have been thrown over the side, and maybe some of us would have gone with him.

For all the good we did later we might as well have done just that.

When we left Port Said we headed north towards Crete, intending to put the German air force at Rhodes on alert, and then we turned back towards Alexandria. This confused the Germans a little but not a great deal. The landing party pressed on along the coast towards Tobruk, all on schedule and waiting for the signal.

Then Laurel and Hardy took over. The Commandos of the Long Range Desert Group had successfully wriggled through the Tobruk Defence Perimeter but the Officer in charge of calling in the M.T.B.s and landing craft lost his signal lamp and tried to make do with a small flash lamp which the German defenders locked onto while the invading forces could not see it. Daft, isn't it? We could not believe it either but that is what happened, so they told us later.

The two Tribal class destroyers went in to land their troops but the first of them was caught in the beams of a dozen searchlights and used by the shore batteries for target practice. Her companion tried to tow her away without much hope and was ordered by Captain 'D' to get himself out of it.

When word came through that the leader of the Long Range Desert Group forces had been killed along with most of his men the Commander-in-Chief ordered the recall of the landing forces. Some of the Royal Marines survived but most of them were slaughtered. Our Captain who was in charge of the Royal Navy forces in the operation decided to send some of our destroyers back to base, including the boats who were armed with torpedoes.

And only after all that did the good man deem it advisable to let his ship's company know where we were and what it was all about — what we had been sent out to do and what an unholy hell of a mess we were making of it all. He then cheerfully informed us that we could now go back to Tobruk to provide cover for the escaping Tribal class destroyer and after that, God willing, we should all be safely back in Alexandria the next morning, and the very best of British. Give that man a coconut!

We carried on with the normal forenoon routine as if we were in harbour. Not even a defence watch, let alone action stations. There was something seriously wrong about the whole thing. It was as if the Skipper, Number One and all the crew had been put under a spell. Did we all go prematurely senile that day? Or were we, somehow, under mass hypnosis? Certainly, when you consider the three years of wartime experience we had known, the way we performed then was beyond belief. What did I say about 'away with the fairies'?

Of course, all these thoughts came to us later. At the time we did not give it much attention. It was just another daft day in another daft expedition. Ours but to do and cry, and all the rest of it. We would drink to it tomorrow!

At eleven hundred hours 'Up Spirits' was piped as usual and my opposite number who was now the Jack Dusty went below to the spirit store along with the officer of the day and the 'cooks' from the chief's and petty officer's messes to collect the 'neaters' — one eighth of a pint of proof rum per man. The grog — which was the same ration mixed with two parts of water — would be served to the leading hands and others at midday.

I was sitting in the victualling office sorting out and pricing up the 'slop chits' ready for a sale of clothing I should be doing the next day if we were in harbour. 'Tanky' was enjoying his stand-easy cup of tea in the middle of getting up provisions for the daily issue.

It was just like any normal working day.

Suddenly there was an awful bang, then another and another and another and then a stomach wrenching, mind numbing jolt while the ship heaved and staggered like a punch-drunk prize-fighter being mercilessly hammered into submission as a horde of Stukas screamed out of the sun dropping thousand pound bombs the length and breadth of the ship which either tore into the hull or exploded alongside with an impact like heavyweight punches smashing into a ribcage. Then they raked the decks from stem to stern with machine-gun bullets blowing up ammunition lockers all over the place while never an angry shot was fired against them. It was a massacre. They too must have thought we were hypnotised.

It was no use asking why. Nobody would have believed the answer.

As I picked myself up from the deck, brushing aside all the cans of fruit and vegetables which had tried to bury me, I had no idea what had happened, but the automatic routine was to go to action stations where no doubt order would be restored and we should know what to do. My action station was in the sickbay flat on the deck above.

There was an unearthly silence where a few minutes ago there had been the endless hum of machinery with which we had always lived but never noticed. Such brains as I had were rattling around in my head as if everything was loose. My knees were knocking and I wondered if the fillings were still in my teeth and if my eyes would ever uncross. But as if in a dream I fastened on my inflatable lifebelt — which did not inflate when I needed it later — and I put on my anti-flash helmet and gloves. Then I put all the store room keys together with a large flash light in the trouser pockets of my boiler suit, which was everybody's standard dress at sea and left my office carefully locking the door behind me.

I turned aft automatically to close the nearby watertight door but I could not move it. The bulkhead had stood firm, but beyond was a black hole where a number of kit lockers, mine included, used to stand. The N.A.A.F.I. canteen was located in that flat but it had disappeared along with its two young civilian assistants.

Shining my torch I could see nothing but a mass of twisted metal, no sign of any life. There was no way through there so I went forward to the stokers' mess deck which was as tidy as if it had not been involved in any part of the damage.

There was something oddly reassuring about that. Three young ratings were trying to push open the hatch above the ladder to the next deck. At first the cover would not budge. It was held down by a mass of debris but we just heaved away until our combined efforts managed to force it open enough for us to squeeze through to the next mess, and what an awful scrap heap it was, a jumble of twisted and mangled tables and stools, mess shelves and kit lockers. There was a gaping hole in the deck head and forward where the cable locker, paint store, and the heads should have been was a tangled mess in which fires were beginning to blaze.

Our lovely new bow had been blown away again and most of the forecastle with it. There was no way out forward. Turning aft we could see what appeared to be a clear way through the sickbay flat which was a foot deep in water from burst pipes.

There was a blood-drenched, mutilated body at our feet and the only way we could tell he was alive was from the faint almost apologetic moan he gave now and then. There was nothing with which to make a stretcher and we had no idea how much time we had so I told the lads to pick him up as gently as possible and carry him to the stern of the ship where I hoped there would be some form of emergency hospital. At the moment we did not know what sort of catastrophe had taken place. There had been no information and no orders.

I was still in a daze as I walked through to the sickbay flat which was my action station — or should be. The sickbay itself was a shambles but I saw no bodies alive or dead. Next I went to the small mess where the sick berth petty officer and his two attendants lived along with us two supply petty officers and the writer. It looked as if the roof had fallen in but there were no bodies there. Jack Dusty was sitting on a locker just outside, the copper spirit measures still in his hand. He had been below in the spirit room when the first bombs hit and had scrambled up through the hatches while they were still falling. Like me, he was trying to gather his wits about him.

It is strange how the mind works at a time like that. All manner of trivial inconsequential questions were rattling around in my confused brain.

I wondered if 'Tanky' had closed the hatches and reported them closed. Whenever we got up stores we had to report to the bridge and ask for permission to open a watertight door. The officer of the watch had a sort of peg-in board which kept track of all the hatches and you were not allowed to keep a door open for any longer than was absolutely necessary. But it would not matter now, would it? There was no bridge, nor any officer of the watch to report to. In any case it was not my responsibility nowadays; what was I worrying about? I wondered who had been the lookouts in the A.D.O.P. and if they had escaped.

I thought about the sugar store. Last year, when that was my responsibility I had been in a panic on discovering that the stock of sugar was less than it should be according to the books. An understanding Paymaster Commander had persuaded the Engineer to agree that there might have been a slight contamination from the oil fuel tank below and three tons of sugar, which had never been there, was officially condemned and thrown overboard. It would not have mattered after all. There was no sugar store there anymore

I heard a shouted order, 'Flood "A" Magazine', and I started to move forward to where I knew were the wheels for performing this operation. The Gunner 'G', the friendly old Warrant Officer who was my boss during action stations, came dashing through to do the job and told me to 'get out of it', or something in words of one syllable, probably quite naughty. One of the words sounded like 'ORFF'.

That was what I needed to bring me to my senses — somebody shouting orders at me so that I could go and shout at somebody else. Shouting seemed to be the thing to do.

I moved quickly out to the port waist where I saw the Gunner 'T' and his fire-fighting party struggling to get the foam making plant through to the fore part of the ship where the fire was raging. This was a huge contraption which they called the 'Sausage Machine'. It required a gang of strong men to move it and I knew they were never going to get through the next three watertight doors. But they had to try. They were not the type to give up.

There was grim carnage. Practically everybody who had been on deck had been killed. I saw a body I recognised as that of a young leading cook draped over the smashed-up motor boat. His lifeless, naked form appeared to be unmarked.

Somebody's windpipe, lungs and liver were hanging on a hook outside the potato locker. That was where I always slung my hammock when we were in harbour. The steady old gunner 'T' calmly reached up for this gruesome object and threw it over the side. I wondered who it had been!

There were bits and pieces of bones and flesh all over the deck. I noticed that my white canvas shoes which, a few minutes before had been paddling in dirty water were now soaked in something very red, which I was glad to learn was not my own. There crossed my mind stories the old sailors used to tell about the gunwales running red with blood. I decided not to look at the gunwales.

The ship was very still and ominously quiet, like a grave. We were a sitting target but nobody gave that a second thought. There was nothing I could do except help the wounded, and I felt very inadequate altogether.

The order came through, 'Abandon ship. Every man for himself.' This was a stupid order and was never fully obeyed. It must have been dreamed up by some desk-bound derision who had never been to sea. In times of distress, shipmates always help each other — it is never 'every man for himself'.

Among the wounded I came across 'wee Jock' — a reservist sailor who hailed from Dundee. He had a deep head wound and a gaping hole in his side. His right foot looked for all the world as if somebody had tried to tear it in half with veins and ligaments hanging out like a bunch of spaghetti; he had other wounds which we could not see. He was conscious and must have been in pain but he could not help himself. My new boss, the young Paymaster, came and took his feet while I lifted his shoulders and as gently as possible we carried him to the stern of the ship. I slipped once on something nasty and nearly let him fall but I managed to regain my balance. This must have been agony for Jock but there was not a word of complaint. As we got him to the quarterdeck one of the destroyers poked her bow up on to our stern quarter and her First Lieutenant threw down a mooring rope shouting to us to make it fast around the bollard. I had hardly got my fingers out of the way when two pairs of very senior sea-boots stepped on to the mooring post and their occupants swung up the wire and landed on the destroyer's forecastle without as much as a 'Me first, I'm a cripple'.

They don't go down with their ships anymore. How naïve of me to imagine that they should be the last to leave!

A running bowline was rigged to the destroyer's deck and we managed to get Jock and a few more of the wounded off without having to put them into the water.

Other chaps were not so well done by, like one poor seaman I saw who used to be my 'Tanky'. He was bravely trying to climb up the scrambling net of the destroyer using his one good hand. His left leg was torn off in a gory mess below the knee and he had a large spike of wood jammed right up his nose. Gentle hands helped him aboard and into the destroyer's sickbay but he did not survive the ordeal.

The chief cook, 'Old Vic', had been badly hurt along with his staff when the ship's galley was hit. The slightly built N.A.A.F.I. manager carried him on his back to the quarterdeck from where he made it to the destroyer's 'hospital' but he died soon afterwards. Some of his mates tried to keep up his spirits saying that they would save him a pint in the Fleet Club tomorrow night. He said, quite cheerfully, 'Afraid there will be no more beer for Old Vic', and those were his last words.

Poor 'Old Vic', he never wanted to leave the ship anyway.

Eventually when it was clear that all the wounded were off the ship, the officers who had stayed aboard ordered us to jump. Somehow, we were reluctant to leave the old hulk; it felt like desertion. This had been our home for the past three years through good times and bad.

But as usual there was something to relieve the tension. We heard the canteen manager say to the wardroom steward, 'Can you swim?' to which he replied, 'No, can you?' 'No, so now is our bloody chance to learn!' They both survived.

Once in the water it was merely a matter of swimming to the nearest ship. It was not very far away but it seemed an awful distance to me. At one time I thought I was not going to make it and I recognised the Engineer Officer who swam alongside me for a while to make sure I was all right before he splashed off to help somebody else.

Finally I dragged my tired body up the side of the destroyer and fell exhausted on the deck. Then I realised that I had been trying to keep afloat with all the storeroom keys and my heavy torch in my pockets.

Some mothers don't half have them!

When safely gathered on board all the survivors had to be given something to wear and there was a standard issue which the destroyers carried. It consisted of a boiler suit, a set of underwear, a pair of socks and a pair of gym shoes. That would keep everybody warm and dry until we were landed ashore. And what was most important of all to a survivor — a tot of rum.

All the first aid books I had read advised us never to give the patient alcohol in time of stress or shock, but the issue of a tot of rum to survivors of a sunken ship was normal procedure. I have served up quite a few tots on such occasions and I never heard anybody complain about it.

I noticed that few of the survivors appeared to be practising teetotals, either.

The poor old Jack Dusty on the destroyer had a hard day ahead of him having all those extra mouths to feed so I suggested I might help him with serving up the grog, and there was a cheer from those in need when they saw me back in my former role at the Rum Tub.

We raised our drinking mugs to the smoking wreck of a proud warship which had been a tough little fighter for the first three years of the war, defying everything that the Luftwaffe could hurl against her. She was now reduced to a heap of junk having been so meekly surrendered to a couple of squadrons of dive-bombers without raising a hand in self-defence. We could not blame the Whitehall warriors for the final act of submission. We felt ashamed and betrayed, but there was nothing we could do about it now. Anyway — we were not supposed to think, just do as we were told. It could have been worse. At least the water was warm and we had not had far to swim, unlike some of our friends in the North Atlantic or Arctic waters.

It was now the duty of the destroyers to give this tired old lady a decent burial. Sadly, none of them was armed with torpedoes and their four-inch guns had no effect on the thick plates of this twenty-five year old cruiser. It seemed as if the ship, having been deserted by her ungrateful family, had found a defiance of her own and refused to go down. At last the long awaited Tribal class destroyer *H.M.S. Zulu* came in at a rate of knots hounded by Stukas and while the Hunt class boats kept the jackals at bay she fired two torpedoes and successfully despatched the stubborn old fighter to the bottom of the Mediterranean Sea — a fitting last resting place. The Stukas had got her in the end — Hell sink them!

What a pity we wasted all that time and money in Bombay. The old patchwork quilt could have been blown up just as easily as the new job, and we had not done much good since our refit.

It was very sad; some of us were almost heartbroken. Shortly afterwards, as if writing the final chapter, another Stuka attack sank the Tribal class boat and the smaller ships had to pick up still more survivors. What a war!

And what a lot of stupid disasters had been dreamed up for us by those boys in the backroom. Ah well, it was ever thus and I suppose it will always be the same as long as there are playing fields at Eton. 'Hebrews, thirteen, eight', as 'Old Vic' used to say.

After all that we did not even qualify for the coveted '8' to wear on our Africa Star ribbon.

In fact, when the war was over and those new boys within the walls of Whitehall grudgingly consented to award us a bit of cheap ribbon and scrap metal to signify our part in the various theatres of war I found out that I had qualified for all my share on that one ship.

I think that was a fair bit of steaming for a 'gash boat'.

We still had a hundred and forty weary, dangerous miles to travel before we would reach Alexandria and get the wounded men to hospital, so the destroyers cracked on stopping only to allow us to bury a few of the men who had been too badly wounded to survive despite the gallant efforts of the medical staff who never let up until there was no more they could do.

It was Monday, 14th September 1942.

We got back to Alexandria at about half-past-eight that night where the wounded were sent to the 64th General Hospital and the rest of us, including survivors from other ships, went to the transit camp at Sidi Bishr. There I endured what was probably the most traumatic experience of my whole life.

When we swam for it we were picked up by several different destroyers and we had not been able to meet and talk with each other. Apart from those we had actually seen and spoken to we did not know who had lived or died. The 'old boys' of the ship spent the first hour or two raking around searching among the company for comrades. The exclamations of joy when we saw a familiar face was a kind of music I had never heard before. I wish I had the poetry in me to describe those wonderful feelings.

Some shipmates we knew well, others were just acquaintances who had not been with us for very long. It did not matter, they were alive and all so very welcome. Then there were the sad enquiries — 'Did you see anything of Spike?' 'What about Sticks?', 'I think Honest John did not make it' — and so on.

But news of those dead or thought to be dead could not dampen the joy of meeting those who were alive. I have never before, or since, experienced such meaningful handshakes. Of the eight members of my own mess, seven of us were lucky. Alex, a young sick berth attendant, a very likeable and popular lad was never seen again.

That night we just kipped down wherever we could but we hardly slept at all. There was so much to think about.

Next day was all a bit up and down — something like a hangover. Nobody knew very well what to do but the young acting regulating petty officer/acting master-at-arms had to organise the men into messes and collect their personal details while the supply staff, especially the Jack Dusty, had to arrange the catering for feeding and watering the men, not forgetting the rum issue and, of course, it all had to go down in the books.

Most of the men just wandered around. Some went ashore but made sure they were back by 'Up Spirits'. We were issued with two sets of tropical kit, stockings and shoes and a cap as well as an empty kitbag and a hammock plus £2 Egyptian money to purchase bits and bobs from the N.A.A.F.I.

The energetic Captain Royal Marines who had served on the ship since the outbreak of war was busy from early morning. He had acquired a tradesman's bicycle and dashed back and forth to the hospital speaking to our wounded shipmates and going shopping for whatever they needed. Then he would come back to the camp and tell us how they were progressing. He walked around among us like a padre offering help and comfort. He fairly lifted everybody's spirits at a time when it was much needed.

There was a junior lieutenant doing the duty of the officer of the day but we did not see much of our other officers.

The thought came to me that in this transit camp at Sidi Bishr to which came survivors from so many ships — men who had been through a tough experience — I did not see anything resembling a Church, not even the Salvation Army. I am sure a bit of Christian comfort would not have gone amiss at this time. Surprising as it may seem we were not all heathens.

During the forenoon the Captain came to say farewell to his ship's company — what was left of it. He explained why he had ordered the ship to be abandoned and sunk rather than risk the hazardous operation of towing her back to Alexandria. He was probably right but he did not explain why he had thrown her away in the first place.

He then went on to single out and praise one of the three officers who had been killed. We thought this rather insensitive to say the least considering all our shipmates who had gone down with him. They were of no consequence of course. Unfortunately that was still the attitude of most senior officers then which explains why the actions of the Captain of Royal Marines stood out like a shining light.

Some of us went up to the Army Hospital and were amazed and delighted to see how well our wounded mates were recovering. The kindly Matron told us that as long as a man had hope in him when he reached hospital he could come through almost anything.

'Wee Jock', who I had been sure would never survive the night, was sitting up in bed as cheerful as could be, chirping away like a cheeky budgie. I met Jock a year later in Portsmouth. He still had a slight limp, but told me he was about ready to go back to sea. I don't know what became of 'Wee Jimmy', the Clyde R.N.V.R. ordinary seaman who was in 1939 a fellow lookout in the foretop and then became an engine room artificer. I saw him in the hospital but he was too dazed to speak to me and I did not get a chance to see him again before I left.

It was the end of an era. Certainly as far as the late *H.M.S. Coventry* was concerned. It had been three years and one month since we mobilised for war and here we were milling around in a transit camp like a herd at a cattle market waiting to be sorted out and disposed of. We had already been sold, although they had not got around to putting clips in our lugs.

We started to shift around the next day. Some of the lads were sent back to sea right away while others had temporary shore-based jobs until their turn came to be sent home. Three of us — a sergeant Royal Marine, an able seaman and myself, all of us having served on the ship since 1939 — were told to report to the master-at-arms office with bag and hammock. We were marched to a waiting truck and driven down the road, which we had seen so often from the deck of the old cruiser, to the Royal Naval encampment at Ismailia — officially *H.M.S. Stag*. It was our thirteenth trip through the Canal but this time we were doing it the easy way.

We were of no importance now. We were being sent home like naughty little boys who had been caught peeing in their school-bags.

We spent two or three days at Ismailia living under canvas with all the creepy-crawlies it had to offer. The 'Desert Song' may be very romantic if you care for that sort of thing, but the sand does tend to get under your skin — all of it! We met up with some of our mates who had left the ship at Port Said just before we went on our last mission, including my old boss Charlie the chief pusser. Again there were many cheerful greetings and lots of questions to answer.

At the desert camp 'Knocker', a Royal Marine sergeant, and I were both out of funds and had no idea when we would be drawing any pay but we had salvaged our Post Office savings books which some of us kept inside the cover of our inflatable lifebelts (just in case — as the doctor said when asked why a man has nipples). We went to the 'Ships Office' where the young paymaster sub-lieutenant (R.N.V.R.) asked us for some form of identification before he could bear to part with our own money. My paybook had gone down with the ship and I could not remember what became of my identity disc — probably lost when I took off my wet clothes on board the destroyer which picked me up. 'Knocker' was also without means of proving who he was but he stepped forward smartly saying, 'I can identify him, then he can do the same for me.' The rather bewildered young officer who had a queue of noisy ratings demanding his attention just gave in and paid us £2 each which was enough to get by with.

I still have that old bank book, time worn, sea water stained and empty. It has not been used for a long time but I suppose it is a bit of history now. It could certainly tell a story or two.

We were transported by lorry to Port Taufiq where we boarded an ancient Cunard liner serving as a troopship. Just our luck again! Of all the modern luxury liners, including the great ones that we had escorted up and down these waters, when it was our turn to be passengers we were sent home in an old tramp.

As the man said, 'Sometimes we do, and some time we haven't'. I thought of my old Geordie shipmate who used to sing to the tune of an early wartime song, 'She's one of the Gash Boats that never complains'. At least we had our own hammocks to sleep in, sand and all. And we were going home.

Ironically we were escorted through the Gulf of Suez by our old friend *H.M.S. Carlisle* — the last survivor of the original six. A few days ago we had been sharing this escort duty between us.

That was surely the end of the day.

Since we mobilised in August 1939 we had pushed and fought our old, tarted-up ship from the Arctic to the Indian Ocean — not bad for one commission and some of us had been with the ship from start to finish. It had been a long eventful three years, only to be sacrificed at the end of it.

When we thought about it afterwards, we had to admit that the ship had been good to us and she had really been a lucky ship. We had covered a lot of water and seen a fair bit of action, but we had also enjoyed a lot of time off being repaired, and we suffered very few casualties until the final day. Other ships of the squadron had seen harder times than we and had lost more shipmates along the line. Anyway, what did we have to put up with compared with the poor old squaddies?

But, my goodness, we were far older now than we were just three years ago. Some of us, young as we were, already started to show a few white hairs.

Our travelling companions on the ship were as varied as a certain brand of baked beans. There were a number of Royal Naval ratings, chiefs, petty officers and others — many of them former shipmates — and a few R.N. officers, some with their ladies. There were also a few pregnant Wrens. There were Army officers and other ranks — the remnants of some famous regiments which had been cut to pieces in the Desert, including the South Wales Borderers and the King's Royal Rifles. There were a few lady soldiers, among them a tough looking sergeant-major who seemed to be taking care of a number of soldiers' wives or widows and their children. There were a few Royal Air Force personnel, but not many fighter pilots among them.

There was also a whole shamble of cashiered Army officers, ranking from colonel to second lieutenant whom the new Desert Commander, General Montgomery, had thrown out as soon as he saw what a rotten, gin-sodden, dissolute lot they really were — convulsed with D.T.s and utterly pathetic.

We wondered how many soldiers had gone to their deaths because of that lot.

'Gash!' We never seemed to get away from it!

Also serving on the troopship was a lad who must surely have been one of our country's youngest fighting men — a thirteen-year-old bellboy who was already a veteran of several trooping trips. A regular 'old sweat'.

In keeping with their position in life, officers and their ladies travelled first class. Chief petty officers, sergeant-majors and their equivalent travelled second class as did the service ladies and the disgraced officers. The rest of us travelled steerage, petty officers being billeted in the sergeants' mess which we did not care for very much.

There was an army staff organisation in charge of the arrangements for passengers and for some reason they did not seem to like the navy, especially when the sailor lads who had a mess deck of their own were regularly complimented on his daily rounds by the ship's master who asked the Army and the R.A.F. adjutants why their men could not keep their quarters as clean as did the navy.

Things started to improve when Charlie, the supply chief, went to bat for us and pointed out to the Royal Navy officer in charge, who had not a clue, that the R.N. personnel were not being given their full rations. We were entitled to four meals a day but were getting only three as was due to the Army and R.A.F.

Mind you, even four meals per day was still mainly spam — fried spam and dried egg, fried spam in batter with mashed potatoes, spam and chips (seldom), spam cottage pie, spam shepherd's pie, and all sorts of other exotic dishes made from Lease-Lend leftovers. But Charlie's intervention paid off.

The petty officers were then given a mess of our own. There were about sixty of us and we elected a petty officer club swinger to be the mess president; he was the toughest chap among us. He demanded a couple of quid from each man as 'bait'. He then went and tipped the purser and the chef so that the petty officers' and ratings' messes were given larger portions of food at meal times — even spam was better if it filled your belly. He also bought a stock of alcohol to set up our own bar which kept us going until the end of the trip, after all the other bars had sold out. The journey became more interesting after that.

Our first port of call was Durban — the South African town renowned for its hospitality to British servicemen. Here we met up with some more of our old mates who had left the ship a couple of weeks earlier. They had been travelling home in the P&O liner/troopship *Orcades* which had been torpedoed and sunk by a U-boat off Madagascar. All the passengers had got away safely except my old friend Sam — the gentlemanly old wardroom steward who had been a friend since the days of Sullom Voe. Nobody could understand why he had left his lifeboat station when there was plenty of time to get off the ship.

I was sad to learn of Sam's death. When we were in Sullom Voe all that time ago there were three men from the ship who used to go into Lerwick every day and became well known to the staff of Henry's Café who looked forward to their visits. They were Alf the N.A.A.F.I. manager, 'Sticks' the ship's postman, and Sam the chief wardroom steward. Alf had left the ship a couple of years ago and had lost his life on a Malta convoy. 'Sticks' was one of our casualties on the final day and now Sam, who must have thought he was safe at last, had gone down on his way home. These were all time-served men having their second go at the blasted Huns. Damn Adolph Schickelgruber and the Devil rot them that begat him!

Durban was a Naval Base so I took my fellow survivor to the clothing store to see what we could scrounge in the way of clothing. I did not fancy the idea of landing in England in the dead of winter wearing tropical shorts. I really did not have the knees for it. It was a pity about me!

I was given a thin blue serge suit, black shoes and socks, some underwear and a couple of white shirts, collars and a tie, also a light raincoat and a sturdy, Service issue suitcase. I did not have much to put in the suitcase but it came in handy for use as a seat during the long journey home in a crowded train. The other lad got a full outfit of 'Square Rig'. The shoes were roughly made of buffalo hide and I have had corns and calluses ever since. Still, at least I am able to walk.

I never did get the rest of my kit made up and I am still looking for my survivor's leave.

We stayed three days in Durban and then went on to Port Elizabeth where we spent another two days before rounding the Cape of Good Hope on our way home. I was fairly travelling the world, as the recruiting posters had told me I should do.

Up by the 'Cape' we found ourselves in the company of a number of small sailing craft plying their trade up and down the west coast of Africa. One of the troopship's officers loftily informed us that they were 'windjammers'. A Dorset-bred, time-served petty officer (other) whom we had nicknamed 'Plum' — because that was the title he affectionately gave to everybody enjoying the pleasure of his conversation — remarked that in his seafaring ignorance he had always believed that a 'wind jammer' was a turd with a knot in it!

We hugged the coast of Africa most of the way as we steamed on, sometimes in convoy, sometimes on our own. We anchored for a few hours in the West African port of Freetown in Sierra Leone where we watched the natives diving to retrieve coins thrown from the ship. There were sharks about but nobody seemed to care.

On the ship there was not much work for us to do apart from keeping ourselves and our living quarters clean and tidy. There were morning parades, boat drill, Captain's rounds, Sunday Divisions and prayers. Some of the R.N. seamen were called upon to man the ship's defences — mainly a few machine-guns. Whether or not they were trained gunners did not seem to matter.

Others had duties as night time lookouts and their main occupation seemed to be keeping a wary eye on erring couples who fondly imagined that their clandestine embraces went unobserved. There were always plenty of volunteers for this duty. I never knew you could have so much fun without laughing!

We provided as much entertainment as we could among ourselves — concerts, pantomimes, lectures, songs and recitations, and the occasional physical effort like a tug-of-war. We also carried out a 'crossing the line' ceremony, blissfully ignoring the possibility that we could, at any time, be under observation by a trailing submarine — German or Japanese. Nobody cared any more.

We seemed to have switched off the war, as if we were browned off with the whole subject. Maybe we would think about it tomorrow — or the next day.

Our travelling companions among the fair sex kept much to themselves. Most of them were young widows with children. There was one very 'pushy' lady who must have had a massive wardrobe with her. She seemed to wear a different outfit every time she came on deck One day she wore a pair of deep blue, wide legged, silk slacks and while she was bending down attending to her child in his cot the slacks clung to her figure in a rather unflattering manner causing one of the sailors to remark, 'She don't half yaffle trousers.'

A chap with whom we had struck up a friendship was a warrant officer in the King's Royal Rifles Regiment and he was one of the few survivors after his comrades had been slaughtered in the African Desert. He was a welcome visitor to our petty officers' mess and rarely used his own bar. One day he came to tell us that the Eighth Army had won a great victory at El Alamein and the Germans were in full retreat.

This big, tough, jovial soldier had tears in his eyes when he exclaimed how he wished his mates could have lived to see this day. We knew the feeling!

We steamed steadily on, not much faster than the ships we had tried to speed up through the Kaso Straits which seemed such a long time ago.

After we came north from Freetown we began to realise how much our blood had thinned down during the past two years. We felt the air getting colder, the sky was darker and more angry. Soon we could feel the North Atlantic swell as we steamed out beyond Ireland and into the western approaches.

It had taken us two months for our journey back to our homeland. We had been less than two weeks on the way out there.

We reached Liverpool during the forenoon in the early part of December. It was cold. We tied up at the Customs pier in Gladstone Dock. There was a dockers' strike on at the time but it was only a 'go slow' so we did not notice the difference. The dockers were demanding improvements on working conditions and I could not help thinking of former shipmates, who were rotting in jail, because their nerves had cracked under the remorseless pressure of the convoys.

We had lunch aboard the ship. This must have been the last of the spam since we got two helpings. We had to wash up the dishes in cold salt water because everything seemed to be switched off as soon as the ship docked.

Cunard did not waste money on trivialities — there was a war on, you know!

After dinner we carried our belongings ashore to the Customs shed where we awaited the attention of the Excise men who chalked crosses on our kit to denote that we were not carrying more than the regulation allowance of duty-free cigarettes, and then we were left alone with our thoughts.

Some time later a fleet of Royal Navy trucks came for us and took us to Lime Street Station where we unloaded our baggage on to trolleys in the hope that it would still be there when we came back. We did not worry so much about theft but your luggage could just as easily be shipped out to Timbuktu if you did not watch it.

We were given rail tickets to our home ports and a meal voucher which bought us a plate of bangers and mash in the station buffet. The special train for Portsmouth was scheduled to leave at midnight so we had a chance to see some of the ruins of the town while we waited. It was awful to see how the folks back home had suffered while we were living it up abroad.

The train was packed and I was one of the lucky ones who had to stand most of the way but I did not mind at all. I suddenly began to realise that I was truly on my way home.

We were met at Portsmouth station by R.N. transport which took us to

H.M.S. Victory Barracks in time for a breakfast of fried sausages and a hunk of coarse bread. So this was how the other half lived nowadays? We still had a lot to learn, and it was not going to be over by this Christmas either! Ah well it did look as though I should be spending this Christmas at home for the first time in five years.

After breakfast there was the usual hassle of walking around and waiting while all sorts of things had to be seen to — report to this office — report to that office, plenty of saluting and all the rest of it. I had been spared all this carry-on for the past three years. I still preferred being at sea.

The Chatham Depot ratings which included the London R.N.V.R. lads, and others who belonged to the Devonport Division, had already been sent to their home stations and I did not meet up with any of them again. I did not see many of the Portsmouth ratings again either, but I was shipmates with three of them on an aircraft-carrier before the war ended.

I was victualled into the petty officers' mess where I had my rum ration and dinner and stored away my kitbag and hammock. The petty officers' mess was a grand palace compared to the cramped quarters I had lived in since attaining that august position in life.

I collected a new paybook and a liberty ticket for four weeks foreign service leave. This was the maximum amount of leave we were allowed no matter how long we had been away. I also drew six weeks pay with the assurance that anything else I was due would be settled up later. They did not say how much later!

I was given a railway warrant and some ration coupons and after dinner I set off to catch the early afternoon train to London for the first part of the journey home.

I was shocked to see the state of Portsmouth town which had been bombed repeatedly since the war began. Many of the well-known buildings had been blown to bits and cleared away, among them most of the multi-storeys and office blocks. There was still part of a ruined building that had once been the grand variety theatre known as the Portsmouth Hippodrome which used to house all the top shows direct from London. Also gone was Aggie Weston's which had been a great place for moneyless young sailors who could get a free cup of tea and a carry on in return for a few inspiring songs of praise. One famous place of entertainment removed from the landscape was a public house which used to be patronised by clientele of a 'different persuasion' causing the old sailors to rename it 'The Flaming Armhole' or something similar. Well, that's what it sounded like to me!

The Luftwaffe were no respecters of person.

It was more than three years since last I travelled up the line from dear old 'Pompey'. Then the trains were clean, roomy and running on time. How different it was now! I managed to arrive at the Waterloo terminal eventually already beginning to feel as if I had actually been in the battle of that famous name. Then I suffered the endurance test of the teeming London underground to get to St. Pancras station where I had to fight my way on to a slow, crowded, tired looking locomotive for the journey further north. It is little wonder that they had to canonise Mister Pancras, he must have been something of a Saint to put up with an oncarry like that.

Puffing along, minding our own business we had to stop engines whenever there were air raids in the vicinity but I had no idea what I was supposed to do if we were attacked. I did see warning notices telling everybody to keep his hands away from the communication cord and not to flush the toilet while the train was standing (or the occupant sitting presumably) but they did not seem to have anything to do with particular circumstances. I parted company with the rolling stock just after midnight when I was decanted to a lonely, unlit platform. It was wide open to the skies after being on the receiving end of a recent bombing and I saw no sign of human activity anywhere. It was very different to the bustling establishment I remembered from several winters ago and I began to wonder if I had got off at the right landing stage. I realised that all the town names and road signs had been covered up to confuse the enemy but I was sure the Germans knew I was there. The Arabs would have told them!

It was too late in the day to look for public transport, if such amenities still existed, and I was not in the mood for hitch-hiking the ten miles home like I used to do, so I just had to hang around the cold, wet buildings all night. The empty waiting room was unlocked but it provided neither light nor fire and the uniform clothing I had acquired in South Africa was not very suitable for this climate. My body was thinking about warmer places.

A starry sky helped me find my way to the 'gentlemen's' where my artistic senses gave vent to the opinion that the loss of its roof had not exactly enhanced the general decor but it had certainly done wonders for the hygiene of the surroundings. Fortunately, I had no particular reason for wishing to sit down and although my fingers were numb with cold I managed to keep the situation well in hand!

At six o' clock in the morning I was feeling very much in need of a change of scenery and I decided to take a steady stroll to the local omnibus station which, to the best of my recollection, was about a mile away — if it was still there. I was pretty sure that the first bus out would be unlikely to leave for several hours yet, but I reckoned anything would be better than standing around here like a heap of old clothes waiting to be collected for a jumble sale.

It was raining but what cared I for such blessings?

By the time I had dragged my poor old feet to the departure terminal I was wet, cold, tired, hungry and not altogether full of the joys of Spring but all the fears and frustrations of the past three years lifted from my weary shoulders when I saw a coach labelled for my home town all flashed up and ready to steam out.

I went to step aboard but I was halted by the imperious arm of a diminutive male person wearing the uniform of a bus conductor. He even sported a small 'toothbrush' moustache but, like that other fellow, he was still a shorthouse. After a spellbinding pause while he made an effort to capture and hold the attention of his coughing and spluttering, hate having to get up, Woodbine-devastated congregation he spoke, solemnly and majestically, with all the command and authority of a demoted, temporary, acting, unpaid lance-corporal in a 'Blind Hundred' about to be disbanded platoon:—

'*You* can't come on *this* bus. It's for *War Workers* only!'

The Last Chapter

Old *Coventry* we leave you to your fate.
Three years you've been our faithful servant, yet
It seems, when comes the time you have most need
Of us, we can but leave you there to bleed

You suffered other hurts but always then
We bandaged up your wounds and fought again.
From Arctic chill to torrid Egypt sun
Your battered plates defied the rabid Hun.

Tormented, trampled, strength you always found.
But now at last you're dealt a mortal wound.
Your useful days are done. 'They' think it best
That we sail on while you are put to rest.

Go then, beneath the waves as ordered to.
Our mates who died with you will be your crew.

Jack Dusty